Mindful Eating

Develop a Better Relationship with Food through Mindfulness, Overcome Eating Disorders (Overeating, Food Addiction, Emotional and Binge Eating), Enjoy Healthy Weight Loss without Diets

By Nathalie Seaton

© **Copyright 2021 - All rights reserved.**

The content contained within this book may not be reproduced, duplicated or transmitted without direct written permission from the author or the publisher.

Under no circumstances will any blame or legal responsibility be held against the publisher, or author, for any damages, reparation, or monetary loss due to the information contained within this book, either directly or indirectly.

Legal Notice:

This book is copyright protected. It is only for personal use. You cannot amend, distribute, sell, use, quote or paraphrase any part, or the content within this book, without the consent of the author or publisher.

Disclaimer Notice:

Please note the information contained within this document is for educational and entertainment purposes only. All effort has been executed to present accurate, up to date, reliable, complete information. No warranties of any kind are declared or implied. Readers acknowledge that the author is not engaged in the rendering of legal, financial, medical or professional advice. The content within this book has been derived from various sources. Please consult a licensed professional before attempting any techniques outlined in this book.

By reading this document, the reader agrees that under no circumstances is the author responsible for any losses, direct or indirect, that are incurred as a result of the use of the information contained within this document, including, but not limited to, errors, omissions, or inaccuracies.

Table of Contents

INTRODUCTION 8

CHAPTER 1: THE SCIENCE OF EATING 12

A BIOLOGICAL LOOP 13
REASONS TO EAT 14
THE WAY WE EAT 15
A SCIENTIFIC DILEMMA 20
MINDFUL EATING ENCOURAGES HEALTHY EATING 24

CHAPTER 2: UNHEALTHY EATING BEHAVIORS 25

SIGNS OF A POOR DIET 26
BAD EATING HABITS 29
POOR EATING AFFECTS YOUR HEALTH 40
ARE YOU EATING MINDLESSLY? 44

CHAPTER 3: MINDFUL EATING MATTERS 46

PSYCHOLOGY AND MINDFUL EATING 46
SCIENCE AND MINDFUL EATING 50
THE IMPORTANCE OF MINDFUL EATING 51
CHARACTERISTICS OF MINDFUL EATING 54
MINDFUL EATING QUESTIONNAIRE 54
PREPARE TO BE A MINDFUL EATER 57

CHAPTER 4: BENEFITS OF MINDFUL EATING 59

BODY BENEFITS 59
OVERCOMING FOOD BATTLES 61
MENTAL HEALTH BENEFITS 64
FOOD-RELATED BENEFITS 67
EFFICACY OF MINDFUL EATING 70
IT'S TIME FOR ACTION 71

CHAPTER 5: PRINCIPLES OF MINDFUL EATING ... 72
- The Mindful Eating Cycle ... 73
- The Essence of Mindful Eating ... 77
- Helpful Tools ... 82
- Mindful Eating For Children ... 87
- Ready for Mindful Eating ... 91

CHAPTER 6: MAKE MINDFUL EATING A HABIT ... 93
- Mindful Eating Activities ... 93
- Tips and Strategies ... 106
- You Can Do It ... 110

CHAPTER 7: COPING STRATEGIES INSTEAD OF EATING . 112
- Mindfulness ... 113
- Meditation ... 114
- Journal ... 121
- Make Small Changes ... 123
- Take Five ... 126
- Do Something Else ... 127
- Towards a Positive Future ... 133

CHAPTER 8: MINDFULNESS AND EATING DISORDERS ... 134
- Binge Eating ... 134
- Emotional Eating ... 142
- Beat Eating Disorders ... 150

CHAPTER 9: MINDFUL EATING AND WEIGHT LOSS ... 152
- Mindful Eating Versus Dieting ... 153
- Weight Loss Versus Well-Being ... 156
- Overeating Triggers ... 158
- Practical Mindful Eating Tips for Weight Loss ... 160
- Mindful Eating During Holidays ... 166
- A New You ... 168

CHAPTER 10: FAQ..169
CONCLUSION..178
REFERENCES...184

YOUR FREE GIFTS

As a way of saying thanks for your purchase and to help you along your journey towards developing healthier eating habits, we've created free bonus resources that will help you get the best possible results:

Free bonus #1: 30 Common mistakes that can keep you from losing weight
Do you make any of them?

Free bonus #2: The 25 Healthiest Foods You Can Buy for $5 or Less
Eat healthier without breaking the bank

Free bonus #3: Atkins carb counter
Know how many carbs are in the foods you eat

Free bonus #4: Intermittent Fasting for Weight Loss
A beginners guide for women & men to lose your body fat healthy and simply

Free bonus #5: Clean Eating
Staying healthy in a simple way

To get your bonuses, go to

http://bit.ly/NathalieSeaton

Or scan with your camera

Introduction

People come in all shapes and sizes and have their own history with food. They might be underweight, overweight, short, or tall. The media is flooded with advice on eating for specific body shapes, the best exercises, and the latest diet, but many people still have food battles. Regardless, the one constant for every person is that they have to eat, but the bigger question is why a person eats the way they do.

Eating habits are rooted in lifestyle and personality. The best way to consider eating habits is to think about the way you eat. Here are a few stories from other people regarding their eating patterns:

"I have always been a busy person running my own business, looking after the children, and taking part in several sports. I grab some quick snacks like carrot sticks or protein bars to keep me going, but I know I don't eat enough. When I do get time to myself, I will eat anything that is available, doesn't matter if it is bad or good. Afterward, I feel bad." - Amber, 42

"As children, my mother would dish up our food and we would eat every meal at the table. My parents were very strict, and we had to eat everything on our plates before we could get up from the table. I remember feeling full before I could finish my plate but I didn't have a choice of when to stop eating. This stretched my appetite, and I continued to eat larger portions as an adult. Now, I am overweight and wish I could change my situation." - Peter, 33

"I eat whenever I become stressed or emotional. I have been on too many diets to count and stick to them quite well, except when something bad happens. Then everything goes out the window, and I go back to my bad habits." - Mary, 27

Do you recognize yourself in the thoughts shared by Amber, Peter, and Mary?

So many people are trying to lose weight, gain weight, or improve their eating habits. It isn't easy, but change is possible. There is a way to consume food in a healthy way, without any feelings of guilt or shame, and enjoy it too! This method is mindful eating.

Mindfulness increases your awareness of the moment you are in and improves your appreciation of a current state. Mindful eating is an extension of this concept. It allows you to immerse yourself in eating so that you can nourish your body and your soul. Mindful eating creates an appreciation for food, how it is grown and produced, and the eating process. During this time, you become more aware of your role in the context of food.

Mindful eating is not a diet plan—it is a lifestyle. With mindful eating, you become aware of the food experience through active participation. It allows you to view yourself in a different light while improving your relationship with food. Mindful eating is about appreciating every food moment, the benefit it brings to your body, and how it makes you feel. Becoming a mindful eater enables you to reduce food anxiety, deal with your emotions, and gives you the control rather than having food control you. It is suitable for the whole family because it isn't a diet that eliminates foods or restricts calorie intake.

Once you learn how to eat mindfully, you realize there are no right or wrong foods and you can enjoy all food to varying degrees. You learn to accept that you are unique, so your eating experience will be distinctive too. As a mindful eater, you have a choice of what to eat, and the control to focus on only the eating process to enhance awareness. By gaining this awareness, you become responsible for your own food choices and accept that you are the only one that can control your health and life. This empowers you to continue eating mindfully without giving in to your emotions or external influences.

Throughout this book, we will look at the principles of mindful eating, practical application, how to make it a part of your life, and address problematic eating behaviors. Mindful eating isn't difficult, but it is normal to stray occasionally. To make mindful eating easier, we will consider how small changes can have a big effect, so don't push yourself to become a mindful eater overnight. Instead, take your time to master the concepts that are easiest for you before moving onto other mindful eating strategies. Most importantly, this book will teach you to love yourself by looking after your health in the best way possible!

Jan Chozen Bays, an American pediatrician, and educator on mindful eating and Zen practices shares this thought: *"Mindful eating replaces self-criticism with self-nurturing. It replaces shame with respect for your own inner wisdom."*

Chapter 1: The Science of Eating

Eating is an enjoyable activity for most people. It provides nourishment and comfort which may be why you constantly seek food. Few people eat recommended portion sizes, especially if it is a beloved food. It is a huge challenge to eat healthy if you really love a specific food. Why is this the case? Understanding why you eat the way you do is the first step to understanding yourself better and dealing with your eating problems.

Eating is necessary for survival and your brain is hardwired to seek food for sustenance. In previous centuries, people would hunt and look specifically for food with higher calories (like bananas rather than tomatoes) to ensure they could do their daily tasks, but these activities were more physical than they are today. Today, people still choose higher-calorie foods, but the contextual lifestyle has changed entirely. Often, the foods that are the cheapest and are most readily available are packed with fat, sugar, and carbohydrates.

Besides the innate drive to eat for survival, people also forge emotional attachments to food. For example, your family might eat cake every Friday, have three course-meals for birthdays, or celebrate being the winning team with a couple of alcoholic drinks. All of these events make you feel good, and you cannot imagine those events without these consumption patterns. Similarly, you might crave the chicken soup your mother makes when you don't feel well because this nostalgic meal made you feel better. This emotional link to food is something that many people struggle with, but biology does have a bit to do with this situation.

A Biological Loop

Your brain sends signals to inform you that it wants to eat. When this happens, the hypothalamus, a part of the brain, triggers neurotransmitters and hormones that encourage you to eat. So, eating is a biological process. However, eating is something you are taught to do from the time you are born. The act of chewing and swallowing starts when you are an infant, and it provides satisfaction because you are answering the call of the hypothalamus.

As you eat, your stomach expands, and receptors send signals to your brain to indicate you are nearing fullness. This connection between your mind and body is known as the mind-gut connection. The receptors also trigger the release of feel-good hormones which makes eating a pleasant activity. One of these hormones is dopamine that rewards you for eating by providing feelings of pleasure which is why many people eat to feel better. The truth, though, is that feel-good hormones can be triggered by other activities than eating, so food should not be the only coping mechanism you use.

Reasons To Eat

Food is all around us, which means there is temptation and all the more reason to eat. People are eating more because food is convenient, accessible, and scientifically-engineered to make the eating experience enjoyable. This barrage of food information provides a challenge. Are you physically hungry or is it your mind and body playing tricks on you?

In most cases, you can classify your hunger into one of three categories. The first is a physical need to eat. If you are truly hungry, then you would be willing to eat anything. To determine if you are physically hungry, ask yourself whether you are willing to eat a carrot or something similar that is really healthy, specifically if it is not something you would normally choose. The second reason for eating is a desire or want to consume food. Usually, this desire comes across as cravings for something sweet, savory, carb-loaded, or textural. It is an experiential desire and not a pang of physical hunger. The final reason is believing you should eat, such as thinking you must eat because it is lunchtime or since other people are eating.

The Way We Eat

Now that you know the reasons why people eat, it is time to look at food prompts and the way we eat food. The media and grocery stores bombard shoppers with numerous food choices and include all kinds of scientific claims. Unfortunately, a lot of foods that are healthy are in stores either because it's expensive or people favor convenience foods.

Let's see how all these factors come together to help us make food choices and get some insight into how mindful eating can help.

Taste Rather Than Health

Sometimes, people do not naturally choose food based on it being healthy. Rather, people prefer foods that taste good. For example, you might decide to eat an orange because it is sweet, not because it contains a lot of vitamin C. This desire for good taste is something you are born with and develops over time. Being exposed to a variety of foods as a child can make it easier for you to enjoy healthier foods, but in many cases, you will have to acquire a taste for healthy foods through the knowledge that it is good for you. Mindful eating will help you to increase your awareness of food and teach you to savor every bite.

Favorites

Everyone has a favorite food, and probably more than one. Your favorite food could provide a sense of nostalgia or conjure up good feelings, so you might eat this food more frequently. Many people struggle to give up their favorite foods when going on a diet and probably break their diet because they chose to eat a favorite. Having an obsession with these foods will prevent you from sticking to a diet, but mindful eating doesn't require that you give up any foods. Instead, you will learn how to enjoy your favorite foods in moderation while considering your health.

Diet Personality

You are a unique individual and have your own personality. You like certain foods prepared in specific ways, just like you have other eating habits. For example, you might eat three meals a day based on a meal plan or prefer six smaller meals per day. Changing your diet personality to fit in with a new diet is a challenge because you are used to doing things in a specific manner. Mindful eating does not require adaptations to your diet personality. It teaches you to use your diet personality mindfully, which is the key to weight management success.

Visual Consumption

The saying, "eating with your eyes" is one you may be familiar with. It means that looking at food already awakens your senses and makes you want to eat the food you see. Think about restaurant menus containing pictures, watching cooking shows, and food displays in the store. You naturally gravitate to the plates with visual appeal and find yourself salivating by simply looking at the dish. Food that looks good is a temptation, but mindful eating will help you decide whether you really need to eat that food or whether you can replicate a dish in a healthier way.

Choices Galore

Have you ever been to a buffet restaurant, or maybe had a buffet at a wedding? There are so many choices that you don't know what to pick, so you take a bit of everything. Think about the last buffet for a moment. If you took two types of meat, rice, roasted potatoes, three veg, salad, and two desserts, then you have eaten about three times the number of calories than you should in an average meal. This amounts to approximately the same number of calories as you would eat on an average day because buffets make you dish up larger portions too. In contrast, sticking with a few basic foods at mealtimes and avoiding buffets as far as possible is best. Mindful eating allows you to exercise control when choosing which foods to eat and enables you to eat less of the items on a buffet.

Convenience and Cost

People rush from one thing to the next, be it work, school, sports, or hobbies. This constant rushing and feeling tired limits your time and makes it difficult to think about and cook proper food. It is much easier to grab a coffee and bagel on the way to work, soda with a takeout meal, a sugary snack during your lunch break, and grab a frozen convenience meal on the way home. Sometimes, people feel that these options are faster and cheaper than making meals from scratch, but this is not always the case. With mindful eating, you will learn how to choose your food wisely so that it provides nutrition, but can also be put together quickly. If you become a mindful eater, you can make better decisions even when it comes to takeout and at restaurants, which makes it easier to eat healthily.

Boredom

Sometimes, people are bored and need something to do, so they reach for a snack. You probably have several examples of this in your own life which may include eating mindlessly while watching TV or snacking while lounging next to the pool. When you are bored, your mind seeks stimulation and a release of hormones, which is easy to achieve with eating. These activities and accompanied eating are not beneficial to your health or wellbeing. With mindful eating, you will realize that your boredom can be turned into productive activities that release feel-good hormones without a bite of food.

Social Eating

The average person eats substantially more when they are away from home, and especially when in the company of other people. Social gatherings tend to be loaded with food since several people bring dishes or snacks leading to more food than necessary for each person. Giving in and eating more than you should occur through an unsaid type of peer pressure when people offer food, or those around you over-consume, which lets your own guard slip. Mindful eating teaches you to savor the company instead of the food and encourages spending time with people that also make healthy choices.

A Scientific Dilemma

The media continuously reports about the latest diet trend, the best foods to eat, and ones you should avoid at all costs. A few months or years later, you read a new article in the same publication claiming that the food it once reported as the holy grail should now be avoided at all costs. Eggs are a great example of this phenomenon. During the 1990s and early 2000s, reports indicated that eggs are off-limits if you want to avoid heart problems. By 2015, dietary advice said that eggs are an excellent source of protein and can be eaten without cholesterol or cardiovascular worries. In 2019, the egg debate took another u-turn when studies showed a link between eggs and a higher chance of cardiovascular problems. There is so much conflicting information that it's hard to know what to do.

If science doesn't know what you should and shouldn't eat, then how should you know what is right and wrong? No wonder diet advice is contradictory—it really depends on who you ask for advice. There are a few reasons for this contradictory advice including our own food reporting, too many scientific variables and a good deal of marketing input.

Answering Questions

Questionnaires are a great source of information for researchers, but participants don't always answer truthfully. For example, if someone approaches you with a questionnaire about your caffeine habit, it is very difficult to admit that you drink six cups of coffee per day, so you rather select the option that says you drink two coffees daily. The next question could ask whether you consume energy drinks and how frequently. You don't want to admit you drink one energy drink daily because you think it will reflect badly on you.

The problem with answering questionnaires in this way is that you are distorting the research results. If the researchers surveyed 500 people and half of them changed their answers favorably, then that research is no longer useful, but the researchers don't know when someone isn't telling the truth. They analyze the data from this research and use it to provide dietary advice, but obviously, this advice has issues. No wonder some research claims seem ludicrous when reading articles. If you ever do participate in research, then ensure you answer truthfully because you will be helping other individuals just like yourself who look to researchers for dietary advice.

Too Many Variables

To test whether any food is great or problematic, researchers must do studies. A proper research study requires that the researchers control specific variables and compare them to a placebo or control group. It is very challenging to control all variables in a research study. For example, to study the effect of eggs on a person's health, researchers may require that participants eat no other proteins or fatty foods that could affect the heart. This is a huge challenge for participants, especially if they have to take control of their own meal plans.

The other issue is that each person is different, so studying the food effects in one group might not provide the same results in another group. For example, testing in a group of individuals with a body mass index (BMI) below 25 might not help individuals with a BMI over 30. Similarly, studying food effects in diabetics may not yield the same results as in individuals with no health problems. It is crucial that you understand the context of a research study before assuming it is applicable to your case.

Food Marketing

Every organization wants to push the sales of their products, so they turn to marketing to boost their numbers. Some food producers, including healthy food manufacturers, will pay researchers to do research into their products and cherry-pick results that provide favorable results. For example, a wine producer may pay for a study to show that their wine has health benefits but ignore the alcoholic effect. These results are published in the media and individuals seeking affirmation of their food choices will then purchase this product because it is deemed healthy. In reality, the results are distorted because they were purchased, just like manufacturers pay for advertising for other products. Always question the article if it contains words like "sponsored" or "paid promotion."

Mindful Eating Encourages Healthy Eating

Every day, you are faced with a myriad of food choices, and there are many reasons why you might eat. This situation is entirely normal. Turning to research and dietary advice is useful, but may not provide the information you require. The great thing about mindful eating is that it doesn't restrict food, rather, it encourages healthy eating habits. By focusing on your awareness while eating, you are addressing your emotions and concentrate on filling your body with good nutrients. It is a natural way to improve your life without worrying when a certain food will go out of fashion.

Chapter 2: Unhealthy Eating Behaviors

What eating habits do you have that you consider unhealthy? You might consider a bad eating habit to be skipping breakfast, adding extra butter to your toast, or sneaking midnight snacks. The main issue is that society is okay with encouraging a fast-casual trend, and you fall victim to this lifestyle since instant gratification seems easier than taking time to prepare and eat food.

Fast-casual dining may seem like a quick fix when you are running around to get everything done, but it creates three major issues. First, you cannot enjoy your food if you are eating quickly, which leaves you craving more since you remain unsatisfied. Secondly, consuming food and drinks mindlessly means you are on autopilot which tends to increase overeating. Finally, evolution changed your body to release digestive enzymes more slowly, but eating quickly does not allow your body to digest food properly. All of these issues create further health problems.

Signs of a Poor Diet

Most people think the first sign of a poor diet is a changing waistline or clothes that no longer fit properly, but there are many other signs that show up ahead of time. The following signs might be some you have experienced previously and could point to bad eating habits.

Straw-like Hair

When you eat, the nutrients from the food are distributed to your organs to let them function properly. Eating poorly means you get less of these essential nutrients. Hair follicles, where the hair root is situated in your head, are a type of organ too, so your hair gets insufficient nutrition. Starvation diets and eating foods with poor nutritional values decrease the protein available to your organs and hair which causes brittle hair, loss of pigmentations (gray hair), and hair loss. Your hair could feel dry, thin, or like straw if you do not consume proper nutrients.

Skin Problems

Dry, oily, or troublesome skin could be an indicator of poor health. Your skin requires sufficient nutrition to remain elastic and in good condition. Removing specific foods from your diet could result in dry skin, such as when you don't eat any healthy fats. Similarly, eating too much oily food may lead to skin breakouts and pimples. Any damage to your skin could cause premature aging and make your skin look dull, wrinkled, create dark undereye circles, or lose its glow. Eating a balanced diet allows your skin to receive the required nutrition to look great.

Digestive Changes

Digestive problems like reflux, constipation, and diarrhea are prevalent symptoms of a poor diet. Insufficient fiber is the usual culprit for both constipation and diarrhea and can affect your overall health. With mindful eating, you will learn how different foods contribute to your health and bodily functions. You will also realize that there are many food choices that provide excellent nutritional benefits, which means you rely less on chemically produced items to help ease your digestive problems.

Oral Health Issues

Cavities and gum problems are signs of a bad diet, especially if you practice good oral hygiene like brushing your teeth and flossing. Eating too many sugary foods or consuming fizzy drinks causes damage to the enamel of the teeth which may result in cavities. Your gums may have a red line where they meet the teeth or have inflammation or bleeding. These things indicate some type of gum infection, which is another indicator of bad health or nutritional deficiencies, such as too little vitamin C. Mindful eating improves your health by encouraging consumption of nutrient-rich foods while eating less junk food.

Poor Healing

Cuts or other wounds require protein, nutrients, and calories to heal properly and in good time. Eating poorly weakens your immune system, which means your wounds do not get what is necessary to heal quickly and well. Insufficient nutrition delays the generation of new tissues and creates an opportunity for infection. It is best to increase the consumption of nutritious foods to give your body a chance to heal properly.

Brain Drain

Any memory problems or feeling extremely tired could indicate a lack of adequate nutrition. If you do eat healthy foods, then your brain doesn't receive the nutrients it requires to function. This causes fatigue, shortens your attention span, and makes you forget things. Mindful eating will teach you that eating healthily improves your mental health and makes it easier to sleep—it helps you to be mindful of everything you do, so you might find that you change your sleeping patterns too.

Getting Sick Frequently

Poor nutrition compromises our immune system leaving us susceptible to infection and illness. A weak immune system struggles to fight off infection, so it leaves you vulnerable to becoming ill easily, and you take longer to get better. Eating foods containing lots of vitamins and nutrients ensures your immune system gets a boost and strengthens your immune system to fight off future infections.

Bad Eating Habits

Sometimes, you remain unhappy with your body, even when you put in a conscious effort to improve yourself. You might want to put on a few extra pounds to become pregnant or lose a few pounds to fit into a special outfit. Regardless of the changes you make, you do not see the results you want. This can leave you feeling frustrated and unmotivated. The reason for this could be a bad eating habit and one you might not realize you have. The following list contains some of the most popular bad eating habits.

Mindless Eating

Mindless eating is something you might fall prey to. It occurs when you eat without concentrating on the food you are consuming, such as eating popcorn in a movie theater or snacking while working on a computer. You don't realize how much you are consuming when you do this, and you might be surprised that the bowl is empty when you can't even remember taking more than one or two bites. Another problem with mindless eating is the way you serve the food. Purchasing the largest size containers will result in eating more, especially if you eat straight from the packaging. Similarly, placing food in a large bowl or on a large plate makes it seem as if you have very little on your plate, so you will mindlessly eat everything and not appreciate the amount. Being mindful of food requires consideration of what you are eating and how you present it.

Skipping Breakfast

Breakfast gives you a start to your day and helps improve your concentration and energy. You might skip breakfast because you have too many other things to do. Skipping breakfast could lead to overeating later during the day or drinking energy drinks to get through the day. Mindful eating encourages you to do the best thing possible for your body, and that may include eating breakfast, which could help you to lose weight and have more energy in the long-term. However, you could find skipping breakfast beneficial if you are using the 16/8 intermittent fasting method, as it improves energy and concentration.

Nighttime Eating

Are you one of those people who wants a midnight snack, or opens the fridge frequently after dinner? Some research studies found that eating at night may cause weight gain. The other problem is that most nighttime snackers select starches or sugary foods that are high in carbohydrates. Your body needs less energy while you sleep, so all those consumed calories cannot be used productively, and you might experience poor sleep as your body digests the food. Mindful eating helps you to make better food choices and questions whether you are truly hungry, which means you might overcome this habit once and for all.

Insufficient Daytime Eating

Eating fewer meals during the day doesn't mean you will lose weight automatically. You might skip breakfast or lunch, because you are too busy to eat or think it will help you to lose weight, but the opposite tends to happen. If you skip meals, you may find you are snacking more, or become so famished that you consume too much food at night. You might even eat more than you would have on a typical day. Eating poorly throughout the day results in fluctuating energy levels, and may leave you feeling tired. Mindful eating helps you focus on the best nutrition for your body so that you are in your best shape possible.

Not Eating at Home

Buying foods from coffee shops, take-outs, or restaurants is a problem. Not only can it take bites out of your budget, but it also decreases your awareness of food. You might find that you order more than you would eat at home or choose foods high in fat and carbohydrates. Most places prepare huge portions which means you might be eating more than you should. Those extra calories quickly add up, especially if you frequent these establishments. The best option is to eat meals made at home and prepare your own food for work where you have full awareness and can make proper food decisions.

Frequent Snacking

Snacking is a big problem for many people. You might want something to munch between meals when you go from one appointment to the next or while driving. Although you might choose an apple or celery sticks occasionally, you most likely reach for a high-calorie item like cookies or donuts. Mindful eating will change this habit into questioning to decide if you really need to eat and the best thing to eat.

Emotional Eating

After a bad day, when you want to celebrate something, or during high-stress times, you may find yourself eating more. This is a coping mechanism to help you deal with your emotions. Sometimes, people call it "eating your feelings," which describes the situation quite well. Emotional eating frequently results in consuming more than you should or eating less nutritious foods. With mindful eating, you will finally get control over emotional eating and find other ways to cope with your feelings.

Quick Eating

You might have a hectic schedule and find it easiest to eat on the run by grabbing a sandwich between meetings or drinking an energy drink as a quick "pick me up" before heading to the gym. Few individuals who eat on the go make healthy food choices because the easiest option is to get convenience food or to grab a snack full of processed food items. Combined with eating on the go comes eating food rapidly. You only have a few minutes between meetings or while driving and need to eat your food in a short time. When you eat quickly, you don't give time for your stomach to communicate feelings of fullness to your brain, which means you eat much more before feeling full. Slowing down is a part of mindful eating that helps you to enjoy your food and become aware of satiation.

Improper Liquid Use

Drinking fluids is essential for hydration, but few people use liquids responsibly. It is best to drink water since it hydrates without adding extra calories. Think about what you drink on a daily basis. Many individuals drink sugary beverages, energy drinks, or excessive amounts of alcohol. All of these fluids contain extra calories, so mindlessly drinking liquids could become problematic if you are trying to be healthier. It is much better to select low-calorie beverages and enjoy the hydrating feeling rather than the instant gratification of other drinks.

Eating Alone

Life has become a constant rush, and many families no longer eat meals together. This is problematic because you might start eating at strange times of the day, eat too much, or skip several meals entirely. When you eat alone, you tend to take shortcuts or opt for convenience foods and snacks rather than eating healthy meals like you would have if you were eating with family. Make time to sit down with your family, or if you are far away from them, then have meals with your friends or neighbors. It encourages you to spend time together and improves your health, which means your eating habits improve too.

Portion Confusion

How do you decide what a suitable portion of food should be? Do you measure it out in weight or simply ladle the food onto your plate? Most people tend to misjudge portion sizes entirely and opt for larger sizes rather than a recommended daily amount. Restaurants and takeout establishments don't help this process either because they provide supersized portions. Although mindful eating doesn't limit your food choices, you should still consider whether the amount of food you consider as a portion is suitable, or whether it requires adjusting. In most cases, this will happen naturally during the mindful eating process through various techniques.

Junk Food

Plenty of processed foods can be found in takeaways shops and grocery store aisles. It includes any food that has gone through some form of processing, which usually has added ingredients. For example, chips, processed cheese, frozen chicken, candy, and so on. Processed food contains excess amounts of sugar, salt, and fat, and these are all bad for your health. You might not realize what is going into your food products if you don't read food labels. Junk food may contain ingredients that encourage addiction and trigger the release of feel-good hormones, which only makes you eat more. Mindful eating improves awareness of ingredients in foods you select and encourages healthier options.

Sneaky Sugar

You may know there is sugar in candy, fizzy drinks, and cookies, but there is a lot of sugar in other foods too, even healthy ones. Salad dressings, bread, fruit juice, and whole-grain cereals along with many other foods, contain added sugar. Sugar adds large amounts of calories to your diet, but it holds no nutritional value, which means it is empty calories. Take some to be mindful about the foods you eat by reading the ingredients and food label to see if the food contains sugar. You might be surprised about how many foods have sugar and simply making better choices could have a great effect on your health.

Eating Continuously

You might find yourself eating continuously. For example, you grab some risks with your first coffee in the morning, have breakfast, eat lunch, grab something else to eat for extra energy at lunch, have dinner, and eat something small to last you for the last few hours of the night. Constant eating is different from snacking because you eat with the intention of having smaller meals to provide you energy, rather than eating something quickly. Most, if not all, of this frequent eating happens mindlessly. It makes food a crutch for support because you just need a little something to keep going.

Screen Time

Staring at a screen for hours on end can result in mindless eating and overeating. You might work a job where you are behind a computer screen for several hours a day, enjoy watching a series, spend time playing video games, or use your mobile phone frequently. All of this screen time can be disastrous, especially if you are eating snacks in between, instead of preparing meals and eating with family members. If you have spent several hours in front of a screen, then you could be consuming much more when you do get your hands on food. Another issue is that you either drink too much or too little fluids, which causes excess calorie consumption in the first case and dehydration in the latter. Being mindful encourages an overall healthier lifestyle which means you will be eating better and moving more.

Not Planning Meals

The majority of people do not plan their meals. You might shop aimlessly and simply add more foods to the cart. Most of these foods are microwave or oven meals, junk food, or sugary snacks. Even worse, you might be so busy that you forgo making meals entirely, and rather opt for a drive-thru or meal delivery service. Many times, you might blame being busy for this situation. However, doing a meal plan only takes a few minutes and you can shop quickly because you know what foods you require. It will help you save time and money, and your body will thank you for feeding it less junk. Meal planning can seem like a chore, but it is an opportunity to become aware of what you are going to eat and whether it is good for you.

Healthy Food Trap

There are some misconceptions about so-called "healthy" foods. You might drink a protein shake and add some fruit and peanut butter into it, for example. Although all these foods are healthy, they contain lots of calories, fats, and sugars which quickly increases your calorie count for the day. This results in overeating and makes you feel uncomfortably full. Another example is eating a vegetable platter at a restaurant since vegetables are healthy. However, the added ingredients like oil, salt, and cream change the calorie count and you may not realize that the portions are too large, so you continue to overeat.

Poor Eating Affects Your Health

The signs of a poor diet already indicate that unhealthy eating already has consequences. However, those symptoms are minor when compared to some other potential consequences. Understanding the risks helps you to understand why eating healthy food is essential if you want to be the best possible version of yourself.

Obesity

Being overweight is a major concern for anyone with poor eating habits. All the junk you are feeding your body will add up, and eventually, it causes excess weight. This is something that almost two-thirds of Americans struggle with, which shows the extent of mindless eating. Obesity increases your risks of getting other medical conditions, so it is something you want to avoid.

Hypertension

Hypertension, commonly known as high blood pressure, is a big problem, since many people do not realize they suffer from this condition. You may experience hypertension if you eat a lot of junk food, sugar, salt, refined foods, and fried food. Even with treatment, hypertension may still result in cardiovascular issues such as heart attacks.

High Cholesterol

Foods that contain fat contribute to cholesterol levels in your body. Eating high-fat food, especially those with saturated fats, is the main culprit in this case, since it causes excess fat in your blood and affects your heart. High cholesterol levels could lead to blockages in your blood vessels and heart disease, which kills thousands of people each year.

Stroke

Plaque can build up in your blood vessels just like it does on your teeth. It is the result of eating foods high in cholesterol, fat, and salt. When this happens, your blood vessels become narrower and make it more difficult to pump blood through your body. When plaque build-up breaks free from a vessel, it forms a clot, which can travel through your circulatory system. Blood clots that enter the brain cause strokes, which could result in brain damage, impaired cognitive abilities, and death.

Diabetes

Although some cases of diabetes occur with a healthy diet, the majority of diabetes cases are caused by poor nutrition. Diabetes happens when you have too much sugar in your bloodstream or when your body cannot process sugar properly. Usually, eating large amounts of sugar and fat contribute greatly to diabetes, so simple dietary changes can help you address the situation. Diabetes frequently goes hand-in-hand with obesity which is another risk factor.

Insomnia

Insomnia refers to lying awake at night because you cannot sleep. Certain foods, such as those high in sugar and processed items, may cause insomnia, as they stimulate your brain activity and other bodily functions. If you do not sleep properly, then you may find yourself searching for a midnight snack, drinking more (meaning you have to get up and urinate frequently), or overeating at other times. Insomnia leaves you tired and causes concentration difficulties which affects your daily activities.

Gout

Gout is something that frequently appears after eating certain foods, such as red meat, specific seafood, and dairy products, among others. These foods could create a build-up of uric acid which forms crystals in joints like the knuckles and toes. As a result, the crystal causes inflammation and pain since they aren't supposed to be there in the first place. Continuous gout may lead to permanent joint damage—a big problem if you value your mobility.

Decreased Sports Performance

If you want to perform at your best, then you need to feed your body the best possible foods. Unfortunately, you might still choose junk food as a quick-fix before practice or after the gym. Junk food cannot provide the nutrients you need to keep up during sports resulting in decreased performance and fatigue. Additionally, poor nutrition decreases your healing rate after injuries, so your recovery will take longer, which takes you out of action for lengthy periods.

Are You Eating Mindlessly?

Throughout this chapter, you may have identified some of the symptoms and consequences of poor nutrition in yourself. If you are still uncertain about whether you eat mindlessly, then consider the following questions.

Do you:

- Frequently eat until you feel overly full or even to the point of becoming nauseous?
- Eat while doing other things (multitasking)?
- Graze on snacks without recognizing taste?
- Eat as quickly as possible?

- Struggle to remember how the food looked, tasted, or smelled soon after you finish eating?

If you answered "yes" to any of these questions, then you are guilty of some type of mindless eating. Luckily, this is not a permanent situation, as long as you are willing to change. Mindful eating is the perfect antidote for your consumption challenges.

Chapter 3: Mindful Eating Matters

What is the first thing you think of when you hear the words "mindful eating?" Some people think it requires meditation or giving thanks before taking a bite of food. You might associate mindful eating with taking a lot of time or having to sacrifice some foods. This is not the case at all. Mindful eating simply refers to concentrating on the food and your feelings while you eat. It increases your awareness while eating and enables you to understand your body's internal cues better.

Psychology and Mindful Eating

How you feel frequently affects all parts of consumption—what you eat, when you eat it, and why you eat what you do. Feeling good after eating is not a bad thing since you are nourishing your body, but it is the type of food you eat and the amounts that determine whether it is good or bad for you. Unfortunately, many people have unhealthy relationships with food, such as when you eat too much or too little, which means you associate food with negativity. Mindful eating encourages you to view food choices in a positive light by changing the way you make food-related decisions, regardless of your history with food.

Therapists believe that various elements in our past and present may affect our relationship with food. Culture, evolution, family, social settings, psychological issues, and economic status may influence your food choices. You might be part of a culture where every celebration is accompanied by food in excess and it is frowned upon to only eat small portions. In contrast, your friends may all be slim and peer pressure could force you to eat less food. You might also dislike certain foods if you grew up eating mostly that food due to financial constraints or your taste may be more expensive, because you come from a wealthy family. Each person and their eating habits are unique, so don't force yourself to fit the mold.

Psychology considers how you behave including your behavior towards food. All the factors above may cause specific behaviors and therapists frequently help people to overcome food problems by addressing these actions. Weight management requires behavioral and cognitive interventions if you want to succeed in reaching your goal. Behavioral treatment is used to identify your eating patterns and to determine methods that will alter this pattern. Cognitive treatment refers to thinking with the aim of identifying destructive thinking patterns that may contribute to body dysmorphia or weight problems. Most therapists use strategies that combine behavioral and cognitive concepts to help you overcome your weight challenges.

Readiness For Change

Before you can change, you have to be willing to change. Usually, psychologists will work on getting you ready for change first, so that you can understand what you need to do to reach your goals. This may include writing a list of weight objectives and making a conscious decision to commit to this change.

Self-Monitoring Acuity

Monitoring your food choices and weight management progress is essential and can help you stay motivated. Writing down what you are consuming or how you feel will make you more aware of your decisions and help you to identify trends or behaviors. Monitoring your progress provides you with a comparison tool to help you see how far along you have come.

Breaking Stimulus Control

Therapy helps you to break the hold that food, emotions, and events have over your eating habits. This could be something as simple as removing bad food choices from your home or staying away from dining out. Distraction is another therapy that helps to release you from the bonds of food by replacing it with other options such as reading a book or going for a walk. Positive reinforcements, like affirmations, finding a friend to support you, or rehearsing troublesome food scenarios may assist in sticking to your weight management plan too.

From Negative to Positive

A large part of behavioral cognitive techniques focuses on being positive rather than negative. Your thoughts are a powerful tool that you can use for good or bad, so concentrating on positive thoughts during weight management is essential. For example, your default thought might be, "I don't like the way my body looks," but this can change to a positive thought such as, "I am working towards a better version of myself."

Science and Mindful Eating

Mindful eating is based on science, as seen in the first chapter with the biological influence between mind and stomach. Science has also proven that mindful eating is useful for weight management, so it could work for you too. In 2017, the Nutrition Research Reviews journal published several articles about mindful eating. The review indicated that mindful eating tends to "rewire" the brain to break bad eating habits and replace them with good habits. When attached to neurofeedback devices, the researchers found that mindful eaters had less activity in the part of the brain that controls cravings and emotional eating.

Having fewer cravings means you could lose weight through mindful eating. *The Journal of Family Medicine and Community Health* reported that a 15-week mindful eating weight loss study during 2018 resulted in behavioral changes and weight loss for participants. Participants that used mindful eating practices dropped six times as much weight when compared to a control group. The researchers also found that participants from the mindful eating group continued to use these techniques when questioned six months after the study. This shows that increasing awareness can go a long way to changing behaviors.

The journal, *Obesity*, published a 2016 article about a mindful eating study. One group of participants received coaching regarding mindfulness, proper diet, and exercise plans, while the other group got no mindfulness training. The aim of this study was to understand the impact of mindful eating on a person's health, rather than on only weight loss. During the study, mindful-eating participants ate fewer sweets and continued with this behavior when questioned on a follow-up appointment. Reducing their sugar intake resulted in lower cholesterol and fasting blood glucose levels. Even if you don't want to lose weight through mindful eating, you will still experience great health benefits, which makes it suitable for everyone.

The Importance of Mindful Eating

Current lifestyles constantly tempt people since food can be found anywhere and at any time. There are a myriad of other distractions constantly vying for attention, which makes it challenging to concentrate on one thing at a time. Consider what you usually do while you eat—scrolling through social media or your favorite TV show probably has a greater share of your attention than your meal. These distractions and behaviors create mindlessness, and over time, the act becomes automatic.

The issue with mindless eating is that you do not recognize cues of fullness and continue to eat. It takes about 20 minutes for your body to realize it is full, so being engrossed in distractions means you are missing this message from your brain. By the time you accept that you are full, you have already consumed too much food and feel bloated or experience a heaviness in your stomach. This is the main concern with binge eating and can be detrimental if you are consuming junk food.

Mindful eating assists you in concentrating on the act of eating. It forces you to consider whether you need to eat or want to eat. It aids in differentiating between physical hunger and emotional eating. By increasing your awareness when eating, you identify triggers that cause your cravings and can avoid them through mindfulness. It may seem like a huge task at the moment, but there are many tools and techniques that can increase your awareness so that you become a successful mindful eater.

Mindful eating is so important that technologies exist to help you stay on the mindful track. Apps and trackers are a great tool to focus your mind on mindful eating, especially if you enjoy using technology. Search on your preferred app store for "mindful eating" and several options will appear that you might find useful. Select your favorite one and use it daily to support your efforts. These apps assist with determining why you want to eat, why you are hungry, work as food diaries, and encourage good decision-making. Some of these apps track your emotions and provide you with additional mindfulness exercises to enhance your awareness.

Characteristics of Mindful Eating

Mindful eating requires awareness or being fully present in the moment to work. This awareness is indicated through the following four characteristics:

- Remaining aware of your actions and how it affects your body, regardless of whether the effects are positive or negative.
- Using your senses to choose nutritious foods that provide a pleasant eating experience.
- Appreciating sensory responses to food without judgment.
- Being aware of how you feel, physical hunger, and fullness.

Mindful Eating Questionnaire

It is challenging to know exactly how aware you are if you do not have something to measure your mindfulness. A diverse group of researchers created a Mindful Eating Questionnaire, which is a scale to assist in determining mindfulness when eating. This scale consists of five factors with 28 items in total. Each part of the questionnaire is described below with details about the five factors.

Factor 1: Disinhibition

Disinhibition refers to a lack of self-control when it comes to matters of social norms. It manifests as poor decision-making and impulsivity, which may be due to cognitive or perceptual awareness issues. If you struggle to control your eating, then you might have disinhibition challenges. Some examples from the questionnaire include:

- Overeating when you attend an "all you can eat" buffet.
- Taking a second helping of food when you feel full.
- Upsizing (getting larger) meals if they don't cost too much, even when you don't feel really hungry.

Factor 2: Awareness

Awareness is all about being present in the moment and noticing small details. Eating food rapidly and mindless eating usually decreases your awareness and could be a sign that you are not paying attention to eating. Some elements from the questionnaire that show heightened awareness include:

- Appreciating the arrangement of food on a plate including colors, smells, and textures.

- Noticing subtle flavors while eating.
- Noticing how eating affects your emotional state.

Factor 3: External Cues

External cues are anything that prompts you to eat. For example, smelling a neighbor's barbeque leaves your mouth salivating or a promotion on your favorite fizzy drink makes you want to buy it. External cues are a major factor that you need to be aware of if you want to be a mindful eater. The questionnaire considers the following points, among others:

- Taking notice of food advertisements that create cravings.
- Notice when you feel sluggish after eating a large meal.
- Realizing you want to eat more than you should when attending events with good food.

Factor 4: Emotional Response

An emotional response is any feelings you experience. If you are an emotional eater, then this is the factor you should focus your energy on. Scale items regarding emotions include:

- Eating to feel better when you are sad.
- Difficulty staying away from sweet treats when they are in the house.
- Finding a snack to eat when you feel stressed.

Factor 5: Distraction

Distraction refers to not paying attention because something else is taking the spotlight. You become distracted whenever you are doing another activity while eating, even if you think it is something harmless like watching TV. The main points for this factor are:

- Wandering thoughts while eating.
- Thinking about your to-do list while eating.
- Eating food so quickly that you do not notice the taste.

Prepare To Be a Mindful Eater

Eating is complex—there are a ton of things to consider from what you should eat to when, not to mention determining whether you are experiencing emotional or physical hunger. There is so much conflicting information about diets that makes it challenging for you to know what is best.

Luckily, mindful eating is a lifestyle that encourages awareness, rather than having strict rules about foods you can and cannot eat. Spend some time on your own, free from other distractions, and consider your current eating patterns and how you would like the situation to change. Think about how mindful eating plays a role in your future and the ways it could be beneficial to you. Now is the time to start setting goals for your mindful journey.

Chapter 4: Benefits of Mindful Eating

Mindful eating changes your behavior and enables you to experience your health in a better light. It is a great tool for a busy lifestyle and helps you to enjoy food while providing nutritional value to your body. Although the benefits to overeaters, emotional eaters, and binge eaters are clear, it is also beneficial to anyone else who has bad eating habits.

Body Benefits

Mindful eating has many advantages for your body. It gives you an opportunity to improve all parts of yourself. Not only will you see physical improvements, your body and organs will also thank you for looking after them better.

Better Digestion and Nutrient Absorption

When you eat quickly or do not chew food properly, you are swallowing large chunks of food. The intestine cannot absorb nutrients from larger food particles as the passages of the small intestine are tiny. Sometimes, the intestines don't absorb any nutrients because it has insufficient energy to digest food, which limits the abilities of your body. Mindful eating changes this situation. One of the ways you become more aware of eating is by chewing food thoroughly, which means you are eating slower. By breaking down your food, you help your body to digest food more easily. It also improves nutrient absorption, so your body gets a lot more goodness.

Enhanced Mind-Gut Communication

Practicing mindful eating strengthens the communication between your mind and your stomach. Once you have a strong communication system, you can understand what your body is trying to say more easily. As you start to identify your cravings as other bodily cues, you set yourself free from food cravings and concentrate on addressing the real concerns. You are not ignoring cravings as you would with a traditional diet. You acknowledge cravings as a symptom of another problem. A stronger connection between mind and gut also helps you realize when you are physically hungry and when you have had enough to eat.

Overall Health Improves

Your overall health will improve greatly if you become a mindful eater. Although it won't solve all your health problems, you will feel better, be more energized, and struggle less with digestive issues. Studies also found links between mindful eating and lower cholesterol and blood pressure levels. You may feel less stressed and anxious, which allows you to eat and sleep better. Mindful eating decreases cortisol levels too, which is the hormone that contributes to obesity. Blood sugar levels become easier to control and your cardiovascular health improves, so your chances of type 2 diabetes and heart problems decrease.

Overcoming Food Battles

You are probably reading this book because you are fighting some kind of food battle. There are so many different eating disorders and weight issues that you may suffer from, and mindful eating can help you address these problems. Having a better relationship with food is the ultimate benefit you derive from mindful eating.

Improves Weight Loss

Mindful eating may help you to lose weight. We have already looked at some research studies that support weight loss, and it is clear that alongside other health benefits of mindful eating, you could drop a few pounds in the long term. With mindful eating, you consider several questions before eating and immerse yourself in the experience. You will find you eat fewer calories, avoid impulsive eating, and choose healthier food options. It might take some getting used to, but you will succeed if you keep working hard. After a while, mindful eating will become entrenched in your lifestyle.

Addresses Eating Disorders

Mindful eating can help you overcome eating disorders by perceiving yourself and food in better ways. Previous research showed that binge eating decreases if you become a mindful eater as it improves self-control. Other eating disorders improve with mindfulness too, since you use various techniques to deal with your emotions, eating problems (including certain eating disorders), and depression.

Fewer Food Cravings

Mindful eating makes you more alert to your body's signals regarding hunger. You might realize that cues to eat are based on boredom, emotion, or peer pressure rather than physical hunger. Being able to distinguish between these different signals means you can alter your response and do not have to eat when you get a craving. Mindful eating enables you to take control of cravings and turn them into other cues which helps you to eat less.

Reduces Overeating

Eating mindfully means eating slowly. Taking longer to eat allows your stomach to send satiation cues to your brain before you can overindulge. It allows you to enjoy your food while making a conscious effort to eat healthier. Your body only sends fullness cues after 20 minutes, so how much would you normally eat in 20 minutes while watching TV? You might be able to finish a large helping of lasagna, a glass of soda, and a chocolate bar. In contrast, eating mindfully results in only eating half of the lasagna and a few sips of soda before you feel full. Leaving the rest of the lasagna and the chocolate bar greatly decreases the amount of food you eat. You might still enjoy the chocolate sometime, but it could be a fun-size bar every few days.

Fewer Food Hangovers

Overeating may cause "food hangovers," depending on the amount and type of food. Eating too quickly results in your stomach filling up faster than it can send satiation signals to your brain. Overeating leads to digestive upsets and may provide substantial amounts of energy before causing an energy dip. Your body requires substantial energy to digest food, so all your energy goes to digestion, which is why you experience fatigue shortly after eating. Mindful eating reduces the number of food hangovers you experience if you follow the basic principles.

Mental Health Benefits

You already know that the satisfaction you experience when eating food comes from a release of feel-good hormones. Mindful eating still allows for the release of these hormones, but this lifestyle encourages other ways to trigger hormones than just with food. You will gain many mental and emotional benefits from practicing mindfulness.

Increased Emotional Control

Emotions and eating have a lot to do with each other even if you aren't an emotional eater. You might restrict your food intake and feel down about it or you could be overeating when your emotions are unstable. Mindful eating teaches you to identify your emotions and deal with them in a productive manner. You will no longer eat your emotions. You will use food as a positive nutritional experience.

Alternative Stress-Busting Options

Emotional eating usually happens when a person experiences stress or feels upset. The problem is that emotional eating is seen as a weakness instead of a coping mechanism, but there are many other ways you might cope with stress. Some of these methods like exercising or meditating are good ways to deal with stress. In contrast, other methods such as excessive drinking and smoking are perceived as poor stress coping techniques. Mindful eating encourages you to deal with your emotions in healthy ways rather than through overeating. By understanding your emotions, you can identify stress triggers which helps you to find suitable stress-busting methods.

Stops The Fight

It might seem like you are constantly in a battle of wills when it comes to food. You think about what you should and shouldn't eat and wonder how some people can leave half a slice of cake on their plate when you finished yours a few minutes ago. These struggles take up time and energy, but it doesn't get you closer to your weight management goals. A preoccupation with food leads to feelings of guilt if you eat something you think is off-limits, and food restriction only increases cravings. With mindful eating, you consider food in a healthy manner and don't place limits on your food selection. This ability stops your internal battle between eating and emotions.

Building Trust

Why do you usually opt for a diet? You might feel that you cannot control your own eating patterns or that you need strict dietary guidelines. But, the truth is that you don't trust your own food decisions. Mindful eating does not give you a strict guideline about what you should or shouldn't consume, or when you must eat. Rather, mindful eating teaches you how to trust yourself, your mind, and your body's cues, because only you can fully understand your body and circumstances. Once you trust yourself, you gain the power to change your life.

Being Kind

Sometimes, you might look at yourself in the mirror and think you hate your body. You might have feelings of guilt or hatred towards yourself after emotional or binge eating. These negative thoughts will not create change. You cannot beat yourself up with hatred and expect that you will change overnight. Mindful eating allows you to accept yourself at every stage of the eating process and throughout your weight management journey. It encourages you to be aware of your good aspects while focusing on positive gains made through mindful eating practices. You will learn to be kind to yourself and actively seek out positivity for motivation when you face new obstacles.

Food-Related Benefits

The big problem with diets, whether to lose or put on weight, is that they restrict your food intake, and you can only select items from a limited food menu. Mindful eating doesn't have these restrictions at all. It allows you to eat what you want by considering your options and the effect on your body carefully. The benefits of variety and enjoying food are ones you don't easily find elsewhere.

Embracing the Middle Ground

If you have an "all or nothing" mentality, then it could be an obstacle to weight management. You might think you should eat no starches, no sugar, and no processed foods. Although these changes could be beneficial, it is not helpful for your mind or your weight management journey. You might find that you can stick with these restrictions for a few days or weeks, but once you are faced with these foods, you start to binge eat. Mindful eating will help you find the middle ground by allowing you to eat any food you want, within moderation, and through conscious decision-making.

Better-Tasting Food

Mindful eating requires you to concentrate on the eating process and the food you are consuming. When you have this intense focus, you start to re-experience food and appreciate the different flavors, textures, and scents. Through experiential eating, you discover new taste sensations that you might not have realized previously, even if it is a dish you ate frequently. Mindfulness allows you to enjoy food without feelings of guilt.

Greater Variety

Mindful eating tends to diversify your palate, and help you become open to trying new foods. You may find that your new awareness prickles your senses and you want to test a portion of food after seeing, smelling, or touching it. Allow yourself enough time to experience each food or ingredient fully by using all your senses, then decide whether you like it or not. Try new foods several times and on different occasions to ensure you give them a proper chance. You might find that your tastes change substantially, especially when you can incorporate more foods into your weekly menu.

Efficacy of Mindful Eating

Mindfulness is a therapeutic practice that enables you to manage your eating habits better. The strategies used in mindfulness are quite diverse, which allows you to find methods that work for you based on your eating problems.

A Perpetual Loop

Any bad food habit or eating disorder creates a self-perpetuating loop. You feel upset about something, so you binge, eat your feelings, or avoid food altogether. After your eating behavior, you feel bad about your consumption decision which might result in eating again. This loop repeats itself over and over again. During this time, you are passing judgment on yourself.

Mindfulness focuses your attention on remaining in the moment. You start to identify elements within the current situation without any form of prejudice. Mindfulness alters your mindset and enables you to determine the best strategy to overcome challenges and move forward through positive change. In essence, mindful eating will break the perpetual loop by addressing your emotions, and help you to make better food decisions. Breaking this link requires a continuous focus on your end goal so that you stay the course.

Engaging the Prefrontal Cortex

The prefrontal cortex is a part of the brain. It is situated at the front of the brain and responsible for rational thinking. When you practice mindfulness techniques, especially meditation, you strengthen your prefrontal cortex, which means you think more rationally. A strong prefrontal cortex enables you to observe thoughts about food and be around food without acting on these impulses. Rational thinking promoted by mindfulness makes it easier to break bad habits and encourages the development of good habits.

It's Time For Action

There are so many benefits to mindful eating that it only makes sense to give it a try. Mindful eating nourishes the body, mind, and soul. By taking care of your body, you strengthen your mind and regain emotional control. You start to enjoy food in new ways, as you use all your senses and diversify your tastes. The best part is that you can still eat what you want as long as you remain mindful of your choices. The benefits are clear, and now is as good a time as ever to become a mindful eater.

Chapter 5: Principles of Mindful Eating

Mindful eating is something that you have to learn to do. You might be practicing some techniques already, which is great. Understanding the principles and theory of mindful eating can provide you with more techniques to improve your mindfulness skills. Over time, you will become more mindful and your eating habits will change, which makes you a healthier individual.

The basic principles of mindful eating are quite simple:

- Listen to your body's cues regarding hunger and satiety.
- Avoid overconsumption—eat anything you want in moderation.
- Deal with external cues effectively, such as eating smaller portions and eliminating distractions.

These three principles affect every part of mindful eating. Although the principles are few, they are great in-depth. Almost all other aspects of mindful eating can fall under one of these three principles. Many tools, models, and techniques exist to help you implement and maintain each of these principles.

The Mindful Eating Cycle

Mindful eating can be understood through a cycle of questions. These questions prompt the thinking process and help you recognize different eating behaviors. Together, these questions are called the mindful eating cycle, which was created by Doctor Michelle May. It considers six main questions: Why, when, what, how, how much, and where. Let's break these six topics down further.

Why

The first question is all about why you eat. Think about whether you are aware of situational and emotional triggers that make you want to eat, even when you aren't hungry. Consider the reasons why you eat when you made the decision not to eat. Evaluate previous diet attempts and determine which ones worked or why you didn't stick to the plan.

When

The next question considers when you eat. Take a

moment to think about when you usually eat or drink something and why you decide to eat at these times. Reflect on whether you are hungry at these times and whether you can distinguish between physical and mental hunger. Think about other things you can do to redirect your attention instead of choosing food. Consider strategies to help you cope better when you experience an eating trigger. Think about whether your eating cues actually mean your body is trying to tell you something else.

What

Next, reflect on what you eat. Think about your food choices on a typical day, and consider using a food journal to help you identify eating patterns. Reflect on what foods you eat for different types of emotions and why you select this specific item. Consider times when you restricted food, how it made you feel, and whether you binge later on. Think about how you feel when you eat certain foods, and if you are worried about overeating these items. Ponder how your choice of food affects your health, and identify areas that you could improve. Come up with some changes you can make immediately, and the food you require to make these alterations. Reflect on the possibility of eating anything you want while keeping moderation in mind.

How

The act of eating is the next topic to consider. Determine what you eat, whether it is a food you truly enjoy eating, or whether you eat rapidly without tasting properly. Compare how you eat in public with how you eat in private and identify aspects that you need to transfer from one dimension to the other. To fully evaluate how you eat, imagine you have to write a review about the last meal you had. If you cannot describe it properly, then your awareness needs some improvements.

How Much

The next question is all about the amount you eat. Think about how you know you have had enough food and how you feel when you finish eating. Compare your feelings after a meal with how you want to feel after eating. Reflect on whether you consume everything on the plate and how you decide to stop eating if you do not feel hungry. Identify emotions and other triggers that cause you to overeat and create an action plan to deal with those situations better in the future. Consider what you do when you eat too much and how it affects the next few hours.

Where

For this question, consider how you use the energy from the food you eat. Determine what you do after eating and if you use the energy for physical activity. Compare being physically active with watching TV or lounging around the house. Think about how you use your free time and whether it is productive for the amount you eat. Take a moment to reflect on exercise. Identify how you feel about exercise, whether specific exercise is more enjoyable for you, or if you use exercise as punishment when you ate something that you perceive as bad. Consider other ways of using your time like finding new hobbies or starting a healthy habit. Poinder your goals for your life and reflect on how you could use your energy to make these things happen. Determine your self-care routines and how you can incorporate wellness into your available time.

The mindful eating cycle allows you to consider your consumption habits as part of a whole, rather than simply identifying it as a problem. This cycle runs continuously so you can start thinking about any question. Whenever you want to eat or think about food, come back to these ideas. It can help you to identify eating challenges and allows you to build a healthy relationship with food.

The Essence of Mindful Eating

Mindful eating allows you to find the middle ground between restrictive eating and eating mindlessly. To do this requires a lot of self-control and self-belief. You can get results if you continue to be mindful. It might seem a bit vague now, but once you start practicing mindfulness, you will quickly adjust to a new way of thinking about food. Follow the next few ideas about mindful eating to help you in your efforts.

The Food Relationship is Permanent

Food is necessary for survival and it will always be a fixture in your life. Your relationship with food may shift from positive to negative and everything in between, but you cannot ignore it. Start to see food for what it is, something to be enjoyed and nourishing for your body.

You Know Your Mental and Physical Needs

You are the only one who knows what you need. You know the needs of your body and your mind.

Nobody else knows what your true needs are and they cannot fully understand your body. If you go to a restaurant with friends, they cannot eat your food for you and they cannot decide when you are full because only you can eat for your own body and know when your body cues indicate fullness. The same goes for diets and portion suggestions. These are just a guide, they cannot determine when you have had enough, and they don't know when you are hungry. Start trusting that you know what your body needs by tuning in to its communication.

Your Thoughts and Feelings are a Source of Information

Your thoughts and feelings provide a myriad of information. They inform you about what your body or mind needs and prompt you to take action. If you have weight challenges, then you might find that your thoughts and feelings are negative. Sometimes, you even use your thoughts to punish yourself when you are something you perceived as wrong which causes you to feel bad about yourself. Mindful eating discourages negative thoughts and feelings—do not play into your negativity. Instead, acknowledge your thoughts or emotions, and use them as a guide to making a better decision about what you need.

Explore and Understand

Diets expect you to control yourself through willpower alone. Whenever a minor slip-up happens, you feel guilty, which results in struggling with your emotions and dissatisfaction. Willpower alone is unlikely to be effective, especially if you are on a restricted diet. Mindful eating rejects this concept. Instead, you use all eating experiences as an opportunity to explore different foods. Simultaneously, you learn to identify and understand your emotions, triggers, and cravings. You stop thinking in terms of good and bad and refocus on enjoyment and health.

No Bad Foods Exist

You can eat any food you want if you are a mindful eater. Absolutely no foods are off-limits. Accept that foods have different nutritional values and that one food may be more advantageous than another. Any food is acceptable when consumed in moderation, and you can do so without feeling guilty afterward. What does change is your experience when eating various foods which allows you to derive satisfaction from mindful eating.

Calories Count

Mindful eating does not require that you count calories, but you should still be aware of the calorie content of the foods you eat. Consider your budget for a moment. You don't necessarily keep track of every purchase, but you do have a good idea about average prices, when something is too expensive, or when you found a bargain. Calories in mindful eating are the same. You do not need to count calories, but calories do count. They are a meaningful way to remain aware.

Look at food labels to identify calorie values, or find the calories in fresh produce by doing an internet search. For example, the average apple weighs six ounces and contains approximately 88 calories; in contrast, three ounces of milk chocolate has 455 calories. What a big difference! In the future, you might choose apples when you have a craving for something sweet, or you could decide to eat a smaller amount of chocolate. Checking calorie counts makes it a lot easier to make healthy food choices and enjoy food sensibly.

Use Inner and Outer Wisdom

Inner wisdom comes from your thoughts, emotions, and experience. In contrast, outer wisdom is derived from external influences, such as a specific context, or cues from your surroundings. When you become a mindful eater, you become aware of how inner and outer wisdom works together for your own good. You might think about a birthday dinner you are attending later in the week (external wisdom), and decide to eat only healthy foods until then (internal wisdom), so that you can spoil yourself by enjoying a favorite. Your food and eating decisions will fluctuate, but you can use these two wisdoms to guide your choices.

Find Joy in Every Bite

Mindfulness urges you to stay in the moment and enjoy what you are doing. Everything you do is an experience and you can learn something from it. Mindful techniques help to focus your mind on what you are doing which enhances your experience. As you choose your food and with every bite, you use your senses. You might find yourself identifying with a new taste, texture, or scent. Besides providing nutrients for your body, you also feed your soul through experiential, mindful eating.

Life Doesn't Revolve Around Food

For some people, food is the be-all and end-all. If you are one of these people, then you cannot think about a life or event without food. This obsession with food will decrease as you improve your mindful eating skills. Eating is just one small part of your life and you need to find a balance between eating and other activities. You are in control of your life and you can effect change when you realize there is a lot more to life than only food. You will start to explore new activities, practice hobbies, and become more mindful in general once your relationship with food improves. Food is only part of the journey, so enjoy the rest of your life too.

Helpful Tools

There are many tools available to help you stay present in the moment and become more aware of your relationship with food. The ideas above provide some guidance when it comes to mindful eating. The next few ideas provide practical assistance if you prefer a hands-on approach.

The Hunger Scale

A scale can help you to determine the extent of your hunger, and help you decide whether you should be eating. The scale ranges from one to ten and describes several stages of hunger, as created by Eugenia Killoran. Whenever you feel like eating, pull out this scale, and find out just how hungry you are, or whether you are about to eat mindlessly.

1. Ravenous

You feel like you are starving. When you are ravenous you could experience feelings of weakness, be dizzy, or have a headache. You struggle to concentrate and have no energy.

2. Uncomfortably Hungry

You are cranky or irritable, combined with feelings of low energy and nausea.

3. Very Hungry

You have a strong urge to eat and your stomach feels empty of all food.

4. A Little Hungry

Your bodily cues plant thoughts of eating in your mind, and you start to consider when to eat.

5. Neutral

You have eaten sufficiently to have energy, and you feel satisfied psychologically and physically.

6. Satisfied and Light

Your body is satisfied with the amount you ate, but you still feel light.

7. Full

Although you are satisfied, you feel you still eat a bit more. Your body no longer needs food, but your mind urges you to eat more.

8. Very Full

You start to have a tummy ache from the amount you ate, The food tasted so good that you continued eating, even though you knew you had enough.

9. Uncomfortably full

You feel bloated, heavy, tired, and full to the point of discomfort.

10. Painfully full

A typical food coma. You have eaten way too much, like when you participate in a Thanksgiving or Christmas dinner. You are in great physical discomfort and avoid movement. You might consider never looking at food again.

The most comfortable hunger levels range from three to six. If you want to eat mindfully, then eat when you rate your hunger at level three. Stop eating as soon as you reach level six. Sticking to these scale points ensures you do not go hungry while preventing overeating.

Awareness Checklist

The awareness checklist ensures you are being mindful and enhances awareness when eating. It contains six questions, so keep a copy close by whenever you decide to eat.

1. Am I sitting down?
2. Am I eating slowly or fast?
3. Am I tasting each bite or eating mindlessly?
4. On a scale ranging from one to ten, how hungry am I?
5. Am I concentrating on only the food or engaged in multitasking?
6. Am I stressed, anxious, bored, or do I have a rumbling stomach?

Mindful Eating Checklist

Another great tool is a checklist for mindful eating. This checklist can be used to increase your awareness. It may take some time to get through this checklist initially, but it will become part of your daily life soon enough.

Meals

The checklist starts by considering meals.

During your meals, ensure that you:

- Pause between bites
- Become aware of the flavor(s)
- Become aware of the texture(s)
- Take deep breaths
- Put away digital devices

Consider the predominant textures while eating. Are they:

- Crunchy
- Creamy
- Dry
- Grainy
- Moist
- Something else?

Next, reflect on the main flavors or tastes. Are they:

- Salty
- Sweet
- Sour
- Bitter

- Umami (savory)

Snacks

When eating snacks, you should also be mindful. Much mindless eating occurs while snacking. You can improve your mindfulness while snacking by following this checklist:

- Take smaller bites
- Chew your food thoroughly
- Eat slowly

Recap

Once you finish your food, make some notes about the experience. You can make these notes beneath the checklist or use a food diary to keep track of what you are eating and the mindfulness experience.

Mindful Eating For Children

Children who are taught to be mindful eaters are more likely to have a healthy relationship with food as adults. You can start to teach your children about mindful eating from a young age, but still ensure they get the required nutrients for growth. Most of the strategies that encourage mindful eating children are similar to those used by adults. The important thing to remember is that your children are still learning to think rationally and will learn about food from you, so you have to set the example and guide your children.

No Screens at The Table

If you visit any restaurant, then you will be amazed at the number of children staring at a phone or tablet screen while eating their food. This also happens during meal times at home, and you might be guilty of this offense too. Any type of screen, whether it be a phone, tablet, or television, will be a distraction at the dinner table. The same goes for smartwatches or radios blaring in the background as well. Teach your children to eat their food without staring at a screen. It will help them to learn more about the food in front of them, increase their enjoyment, and they will start to listen to their body's cues when they become full.

Eating Together

It is always best to eat meals at a table and as a family. When you eat together, you can watch how your children interact with their food and their likes and dislikes. It allows you to refocus their attention on food when they want to do something else and provides an opportunity to concentrate on your children.

Before your family starts eating, take a few moments to be thankful for the food, or let your children take a few deep breaths. This short quiet time allows your child to calm down and reduce distractions before paying attention to their meal.

Table Manners

Mindful eating requires awareness of everything to do with eating which includes teaching your children about table manners. Teach them how to use utensils properly and how to talk about food properly. Explain to your child that they need to take small bites and chew their food properly. One way to ensure this happens is to ask your child to put down their utensils between bites. Encourage them to excuse themselves from the table properly, and make them responsible for cleaning up any spills they make to make them aware of wastage.

Talk About the Food

Chatting to your children about food is a great way to increase their awareness. You can use the mindful eating checklist and ask your children the same questions reflected on it. Ask them to explain what the food looks like, the taste, and how it feels. With smaller children, and when introducing new foods, you could let your child pick up the food with their hands to fully immerse themself in the experience.

Ask your child about how their belly feels before, during, and after eating. You could also ask how hungry your child feels before they start eating. This makes your child aware of their body's cues and helps them identify feelings of fullness. You could also let your child serve their own food (with your assistance), and guide them in their portion sizes. However, do not force them to eat everything on the plate if they say they are full. Trust that your child knows their body. They will come to ask you for food if they are truly hungry, and you can then help them determine if they are really hungry or just bored. If your child asks for seconds or says they are hungry soon after meals, then tell them they have to wait 15 minutes, and then ask if they still want something to eat. It gives the stomach and brain time to communicate with each other and your child will start doing something else if the cravings are driven by boredom.

Don't Eat on the Go

Do not allow your children to eat while you are in the car or in a rush. Eating on the go will teach your children that it is okay to multitask while eating, makes food a cure for boredom, and will make them less aware of the eating process. If you are worried that your child will go hungry, then take a few moments to sit on a bench and eat something before you go about your tasks. This encourages your child to make time for food and increases awareness of mindful eating.

Ready for Mindful Eating

Mindful eating is possible if you put in the time and effort to be aware continuously. The principles of mindful eating are easy to remember, so make a note of them and keep this note handy whenever you have doubts. There are many guidelines to improve your mindfulness and tools to help you remain mindful. Try out one or all of these techniques and identify which ones work best for you. It will take time to get into the swing of things, so be patient with yourself. Over time, you will see the advantages of mindful eating, and find it easier to incorporate it into daily life.

Chapter 6: Make Mindful Eating a Habit

Mindful eating only becomes a habit if you continuously concentrate on being aware and never give up on the process. The benefits of mindful eating far outweigh the time and effort it takes to turn it into a habit. After a while, mindful eating will become second nature to you and your hard work will reap rewards.

Mindful Eating Activities

Several activities and exercises can help you become more mindful. All of these activities work by focusing on specific aspects of the food in front of you. Through these exercises, you learn to appreciate food and your relationship with food improves greatly.

The Food Critic

Mindful eating might seem strange, but there is an easy way to improve mindfulness, be a food critic. A food critic is a professional judge of a plate of food made by someone. Most food critics dine at luxury restaurants or up-and-coming food establishments, but there are also other places for food critics. Think about some of the reality TV shows, such as Masterchef, where judges evaluate contestants' food or a local carnival where there is a competition for the best food. All of these events have someone who is judging.

You can pretend you are a food critic, and "judge" the food. When you take on the role of a food critic, you automatically pay closer attention to the food, the appearance, smell, and taste. Always have a positive attitude when judging food. Make notes of what you enjoyed about the food and what you would like to try again. This is a helpful technique if you are trying out new food, or when you are uncertain about the dish in front of you. It is a useful exercise, because it will help you identify foods that work well together, or when a dish needs another element, like seasoning or sauce, to help it improve. This activity is easy to do with children as well and will help them cultivate a love for mindful eating.

The Raisin Meditation

A prolific mindful eating exercise comes from Jon Kabat Zinn, a mindfulness expert. Zinn created an exercise to increase your awareness while eating by using a single raisin. It works wonders for mindfulness and helps you to focus on nothing else at that moment. Once you have done this exercise, you can also try it with other foods, if you want some extra practice.

Follow these instructions for the raisin meditation:

1. Hold
Pick up the raisin and hold it between your index finger and thumb or place it in the palm of your hand.

2. See
Pay close attention to how the raisin looks. One way to do this is to imagine you have never seen a raisin before and you want to examine this strange object. Gaze over every part of the raisin. Concentrate your attention on the folds of the raisin. Focus on the ridges that cast off light, and then move on to the hollows that are darker in color. Try to find asymmetrical lines or unique patterns on the surface of the raisin.

3. Touch
Use your fingers to turn the raisin around and explore the texture. You can either turn it around on your palm, or pick it up and turn it in your fingers. Try touching the raisin with different fingers to see how the texture changes. Sometimes,

it helps to close your eyes when doing this step as it may increase your sense of touch.

4. Smell

Bring the raisin to your nose, and inhale deeply. Try to describe the aroma or fragrance of the raisin. Take several breaths to fully enjoy the smell. Take note of any changes in your mouth or stomach while doing this step.

5. Place

Bring the raisin to your lips slowly while noticing the position of your hand and arm. Take a moment to appreciate that your hand knows the exact position in front of your mouth. Open your mouth and place the raisin inside, but do not chew it. Feel the raisin with your tongue, and focus on the sensation your mouth creates from the raisin's presence.

6. Taste

Prepare to chew the raisin by positioning it in the right place in your mouth. Notice where the raisin is between your teeth so that you can chew it properly. With full consciousness, bite into the raisin once or twice. Take note of any tastes coming from the raisin. Continue to chew the raisin fully, but do not swallow it. Concentrate on how the taste and texture change as you chew, and how it feels in your mouth.

7. Swallow

Before you swallow the raisin, become fully aware of your body's actions. Try to identify the precise moment when your body has the intention to swallow so that you become hyper-aware. Swallow the raisin.

8. Follow

Attempt to trace the raisin down your throat and as it moves into your stomach. Focus your awareness on how your body feels during this exercise and after eating the raisin.

Utensil Play

Eating utensils, such as knives, forks, and spoons, are tools to help you get your food into your mouth. Your utensils can help you become more aware, because the way you hold and use these items may make you unattentive. Think about it this way—you probably eat popcorn with your hands since it is easier than trying to stab it with a fork or scoop it with a spoon. Although it makes it easier to eat popcorn with your hands, it requires less attention.

For this exercise, you are going to change the way you use your utensils. These activities are suitable for individuals of all ages, but children should be supervised, especially if you give them a knife. Use these steps to have a mindful eating experience:

Prepare Utensils and Food

Prepare a meal that you can eat with various utensils. For example, a salad or a pasta dish. Serve some of it on a plate and add some to a bowl. Gather up all your utensils, and place them on the table with the served food. You can use any utensils you want, but try to have at least a fork, knife, spoon, and chopsticks, or something similar. You can have utensils of different sizes or even odd choices such as toothpicks or plastic cutlery.

Use Your Normal Utensils

Select the utensils you would usually use for the dish in front of you and take a few bites from the plate and from the bowl. You might select a knife and fork if you are eating pasta from a plate, while a spoon could be easier if you are eating from a bowl. Use all your mindful techniques to be fully aware during the eating process. It might help you to have a piece of paper with you to make notes after each utensil about how you experienced the food.

Change the Position

Keep eating with your traditional utensils but change the position you are holding them in. This step works best with a fork. If the prongs of your fork point up, then you probably scoop the food, which is quite easy to do. Turn the fork the other way around, so that the prongs point towards the plate. You now need to get food by stabbing it and that requires precision. Stabbing food automatically makes you more aware, as the movements are controlled and require your full attention.

Utensil Swap

Try swapping your utensils to the other hand. Holding your utensils differently than usual automatically forces you to concentrate and be more aware since additional signals are sent between the hand and brain. If you are using a spoon, you might find that movements are not as controlled. Similarly, stabbing a tomato with a fork becomes more challenging while using a different hand.

Change Utensils

Use the different utensils you laid out to eat your food. Try eating salad with a spoon or a smaller fork. Smaller or challenging utensils increase your awareness because the movements must be precise if you want to get food to your mouth. Try changing to entirely different utensils. Chopsticks or toothpicks can be an interesting change and force you to pay attention.

Write down how you experience food while using different utensils. Make notes of the easiest and most challenging ones. Next time you struggle to eat mindfully, change your utensils to a challenging one so that your brain works harder. If you are eating too fast then choose a smaller utensil, which only allows you to take small bites at a time, and remember to put down your utensils between bites.

The Mindful Plate

Mindful eating allows you to enjoy food, improve your health, reduce negativity, and avoid unhealthy eating habits. There are many ways to achieve these ideals. Doctor Susan Albers uses a plate and glass to identify the key aspects of mindful eating. The plate is divided into four sections that help to improve your food relationship.

Plate Element 1: Observe

Whenever you want to eat, or while you are eating, observe how your mind and body respond to the situation. Notice what is happening with your body, such as having a rumbling stomach, feeling very hungry, or starting to feel full. Consider other physical sensations such as being tired, stressed, or having little energy.

Plate Element 2: Savor

Take note of different aspects of your meal. Determine the different aromas, flavors, and textures. Think about whether the food is hot or cold, sweet or salty, spicy or crunchy. Try to describe the taste as much as possible.

Plate Element 3: In-the-moment

Remain fully present throughout the entire eating experience. Remove any distractions, and sit down while you eat. Switch off electronic devices and concentrate only on the food.

Plate Element 4: Non-judgment

Be kind to yourself when you are eating and do not pass judgment. Mindful eating has no limitations. All you need to do is remain aware. Take note of any negative thoughts that rear their head and dismiss these thoughts while remembering that you are nourishing your body.

Glass: Awareness

The glass accompanying the plate signals awareness. It ties together all of the plate elements and summarizes what mindful eating is about. While you are eating, concentrate on how the food tastes and how it nourishes your body instead of mindlessly munching your food.

The mindful plate and glass analogy assists you in remaining aware during the eating process. It encourages you to consider every element of yourself and the food in front of you. By using these elements, you increase awareness of your mind, body, feelings, and thoughts. This technique is one of the easiest to do continuously and whenever you eat.

Two Plates

The two plates exercise is another useful tool to help you learn about mindful eating. It helps you to identify suitable portion sizes which is necessary if you think you might be overeating or have difficulty with identifying suitable portions. You can try this exercise at home to make mindful portioning easier. This approach is an excellent resource if you frequently dine out, when you think you have been served a too big portion, or when visiting all-you-can-eat buffets.

Here are the steps for the two plates technique:

1. Get Two Plates

Get two plates for you to use with your meal. One plate is a serving plate, while the other is an eating plate. If possible, use a smaller plate as your eating plate. Fill the serving plate with all the food you want to eat.

2. Replate

Move some of the food onto your eating plate from the serving plate. You can decide how much you want to place on the eating plate. Listen to cues from your body, and consider the amount you are most likely to eat. Try to figure out how hungry you are before you move food to the eating plate.

3. Prepare the Food

Use only the eating plate for this step. Cut all the food into bite-sized chunks. Prepare your food for eating in any other way, such as adding salad dressing or seasoning.

4. Eat

Start eating and concentrate on the food in front of you. Be mindful of every bite, and chew slowly. Only eat the food on your eating plate. You can finish all the food on this plate if you want to.

5. Evaluate

Once you have cleared your eating plate of food, evaluate how you feel. Determine if you are still hungry. Identify whether this is real hunger or whether you just want to eat more because the food tastes good. If you are no longer hungry, then you are done with your meal. If you still feel hungry, then move to the next step.

6. Replate

Move half of the food from your serving plate onto your eating plate. Repeat steps three and four with this serving. Cut up the food, and eat it mindfully.

7. Evaluate

Eat the food on your eating plate until you are full, or until you have cleared your plate. Reevaluate your hunger. Repeat steps six and seven, if you are still hungry. If you feel you are becoming full or think you have had enough, then you can push the remaining food aside and stop eating.

Mindful Eating Worksheet

The mindful eating worksheet is the perfect activity if you want to teach your children about this concept. It is suitable for all ages, so adults can enjoy this exercise too. Each section of the worksheet is outlined below, so you can use it to complete the exercise. Use your food diary or a loose page to gather all your ideas for the exercise in one place.

A Reminder

Start off by reminding yourself about the basics of mindful eating. You should be aware of how food tastes, feels, smells, and sounds.

The Experience

Choose a piece of fruit to eat mindfully. Eat the fruit, then make notes about your experience. Alternatively, make a drawing about your mindful experience.

Answer Questions

In the next section, you will answer questions about your experience. You can either think back to the experience while eating the fruit or you can eat something else, and then answer the questions.

- How did it taste?
- How did it look?
- How did it smell?
- How did it feel?
- How did it sound?

After considering each sense, answer this question: What did I notice about this food that I have not noticed before?

Expression

The final part of the worksheet is a space for expression and reflection. Spend some time drawing a picture of the fruit or other food, and draw everything you think it needs to grow. You can include drawings of people, machines, natural conditions, or anything else.

Tips and Strategies

Mindful eating needs to become a habit if you want to make it part of your lifestyle. There are numerous ways to incorporate it into daily life.

Some of these changes are small and easy to implement while others may take a bit more time.

Plan and Prepare

Planning and preparing to eat mindfully is one of the first things you will do during this process. Spend sufficient time on preparing yourself mentally and getting the things you need to make a success of mindful eating.

- Eat one meal mindfully each day for a week, then add more mindful meals.
- Schedule time to eat into your diary and do not multitask at all when eating.
- Check food labels and calorie content of different foods frequently so that you can make sensible choices.
- If you want to eat calorie-dense foods, then choose a smaller portion and use it as a special treat. Most importantly, eat these foods mindfully and do not feel guilty about it afterward—it was a conscious decision.
- Sit down when you are ready to eat and switch off any distractions.
- Take a moment to feel thankful for the food you have before you start to eat. Look at each item specifically and name it. Consider the time and effort that went into growing

the individual ingredients and making the meal.
- Measure your hunger level before you eat something, especially if it is a snack. It might be stress driving you to eat which requires other strategies than food.

When Eating

- Start eating when you feel only a bit hungry since extreme hunger will make you eat food impulsively.
- Only dish up a portion that you believe you can eat mindfully. Remember, it is about quality eating rather than the quantity you eat. You can always go back for a bit more later if you still feel physical hunger.
- Take small bites and chew your food slowly. Put down your fork in between bites, and only pick it up once you have swallowed the previous bite.
- Chew each bite about 30 times, although some foods could require more chewing and others less.
- Ensure that your meal takes at least 20 minutes to eat.
- Never eat from the packaging. Always serve your food on a plate or in a bowl.

- Don't force yourself to eat every bite on your plate. It is okay to stop eating once you are full.

Increase Awareness

- Concentrate on the smell, shape, texture, and taste of your food. Use the first few bites of each meal to emphasize each of these senses.
- Eat a variety of foods including those you would not normally try. For example, choose plant-based proteins instead of animal proteins. Consume any new foods mindfully so that you can experience them fully.
- Use a food diary to keep track of what you eat if this something you think could be valuable to you. Write down how hungry you are and how you are feeling before each meal. Make notes of how your mindful eating experience went and how you feel after eating.
- If your mind wanders while eating, acknowledge the thought and let it pass by, then continue with mindful eating on your next bite.
- Take note of how your first bite tasted versus the fifth and the last bite.

In the Kitchen
- Keep surface areas free of clutter and food. If you can see food, you are more likely to eat it, so pack all food into organized cupboards.
- Make healthy snacks easy to get. Cut fresh vegetables and fruit into smaller pieces and place them in small containers. Eat the contents of one of these packs when you feel slightly hungry.
- Avoid purchasing extra food and limit the amount of processed, refined foods in your home.
- Ensure that smaller plates and bowls are easy to reach—it makes it easier to serve smaller portions.
- Have a shopping list handy to write down any favorite healthy foods so you don't run out of these options.

You Can Do It

Mindful eating is possible. All you need to do is to start. Make a decision today to work hard on becoming a mindful eater. It helps to identify a few easier changes, and focus your energy on doing them fully. Once you master smaller changes, incorporate more difficult alterations into your life. Write out the tips and techniques that can help you best and put them up in the kitchen and dining room to assist you in maintaining mindfulness. Over time, you will find that mindful eating becomes second nature and even things you once thought challenging become easier.

Chapter 7: Coping Strategies Instead of Eating

Deciding to change your eating habits is a huge undertaking. It requires dedication, perseverance, and hard work. Although healthy eating is a noble cause, there is an obstacle. Most problematic eating stems from emotional issues, such as stress, depression, boredom, or frustration. If you do not address these issues, then your healthy eating efforts will be in vain. You risk slipping back into old habits or might pick up new bad habits, such as smoking. The best way to deal with this situation is to cope with your personal and emotional problems in a healthy manner.

Mindful eating has its roots in mindfulness, which alludes to the fact that you should have a heightened awareness of everything you do. Applying mindfulness to your life will help you overcome bad habits for good. Mindfulness also helps you to develop better coping strategies for problematic behaviors. By channeling your energy into productive activities, you learn to deal with personal problems and set the scene for successful mindful eating.

Mindfulness

You already know how to be a mindful eater, so now is your chance to bring this concept into other areas of your life. Mindfulness requires constant attention, and you will need some practice to make it a habit. The basic premise of mindfulness is to become more aware of the things around you and your place within a specific context. It allows you to experience things with all your senses.

Here is a quick mindfulness exercise for you to try by becoming aware of your current surroundings. Set a timer for two minutes. Take a look at the room around you and decide to focus on a specific object. Name the object, then look to the right of the object, and name the next object you see. Continue to do this for the full two minutes. All you want to do is to name what you are seeing, but do so without judgment. Once your two minutes are up, determine how you feel about the room. Identify something you didn't realize was in the room or that you sometimes look over such as a painting that has been on the wall for years. Focus on this object for a few seconds and take it in properly. This simple exercise has made you more aware of the things around you.

Mindfulness can be done internally to help you identify emotions and understand yourself properly. When you get up in the morning, take a moment to identify your current emotions, energy level, and thoughts. Do not pass judgment during the process; only observe these feelings and thoughts, then let them go. Repeat this process before lunch and before going to bed. You can repeat this exercise at any time during the day as it can help you to calm down when everything seems frantic.

Meditation

Meditation is a form of mindfulness because it requires you to stay still while observing the current moment. You can obtain guided meditations through videos and sound clips or you can read up on them and follow the steps by yourself. There are various types of meditations that take from a few minutes to an hour or more. Find the ones that work best for you and use them frequently to help you overcome emotional eating. Commit to meditating for about five minutes a day, and then bump it up to longer periods once you are ready. Below are a few meditation exercises for you to try.

Several studies have proven there are benefits to mindfulness and meditation. One study done in

2013 indicated that mindfulness meditation practiced consistently over eight weeks resulted in lower physical and mental stress, which assisted in decreasing stress-related inflammation and irritable bowel syndrome. Another study found that pain, anxiety, and depression decreases over a one-year period of meditation in individuals with chronic pain. Furthermore, meditations reduce generalized anxiety while improving self-confidence, since participants focus more on positive affirmations and self-love. Additional studies indicate that meditating for as little as minutes per day enhances memory and attention span within eight weeks (Basso et al., 2019; Hoge, et al., 2013; Rosenkranz et al., 2013). With all these benefits, it is no wonder that meditation is an excellent tool to assist with weight issues that frequently accompany stress, anxiety, depression, and other emotional or mental health issues.

Breathing Awareness Meditation

With this meditation, you will be concentrating on your breathing. It allows you to focus on only one thing, which improves your general awareness in other activities. It also helps you to calm down, improves concentration, and relieves anxiety.

1. Take slow deep breaths.

2. Focus on how the air expands your chest as you inhale through your nose, and how it collapses as you exhale through your mouth.
3. It could help you to count as you inhale and exhale, but do not let this distract you from your breathing concentration.
4. Acknowledge any thoughts that pop into your head and then set them free as if they are mist moving through air. Only focus on your breathing.

Loving Kindness Meditation

The aim of this meditation is to help you develop a sense of self-love. It helps you to be kind to yourself, other people, and stimuli that may cause stress.

1. Take a few deep breaths.
2. Open your mind to receive love and kindness.
3. Send mental messages of love and kindness to yourself and the outside world.

Relaxation Meditation

This meditation is fantastic if you need to set yourself free of tension or relieve stress. Your body can hold a lot of tension and you might not even realize it. Tense shoulders, cramping limbs, or muscle aches can be due to stress and emotional issues. Relaxing through meditation will help you to cope with your emotions and prevent you from reaching for food.

1. Lie flat on your back or sit comfortably in a chair. Keep your posture open and do not cross your arms or legs over each other. Keep them at your sides.
2. Close your eyes and take a few deep breaths.
3. Focus on relaxing your toes for a few seconds by clenching your muscles together and then releasing them. Continue with this clenching and release movement through all muscle groups in your body. Relax both feet, and release tension from your ankles.
4. Relax your calves fully, then your knees and your thighs. Spend enough time on these areas as you can have built-up tension in them.
5. Concentrate on relaxing your pelvic bone and hips, and feel them melting into the floor as all tension is released. Scrunch your buttocks together and release this position.
6. Release tension in your abdomen and lower back, then in your upper back and chest.

7. Allow your fingers to relax by clenching then releasing, moving up to your wrists, forearms, elbows, and upper arms.
8. Scrunch your shoulders upwards. Relax your shoulders fully and ensure that you are not pulling them up or holding excess tension. Let it all go. Relax your neck muscles.
9. Purse your lips together and then release them into a neutral position to remove tension. Scrunch your face muscles and release them, then do the same with your eyes. Crease your forehead into a frown, then relax completely.
10. Continue to take deep breaths as you relax fully. Open your eyes when you are ready.

Kindness Meditation

Being kind to yourself is something you should do all the time. It is difficult to look at yourself kindly if you feel your eating habits are poor or when a craving becomes intense. Use this meditation to help you overcome feelings of negativity and to improve your kindness towards your body and soul.

1. Sit down in a quiet and comfortable area such as a favorite couch, in the garden, or on some pillows.
2. Close your eyes and turn your attention to your breathing. Notice how the air moves through your body and the rise and fall of your chest. Become aware of the present moment.
3. Ask your breath to be a messenger as it moves through your entire body and mind. Let it communicate how you are feeling at this moment. Notice the message, but do not judge or react to it.
4. Tune into your breathing again. Find the pause right before you exhale. Feel the negativity and tension leaving your body as you exhale.
5. Visualize a loving presence. It could be someone you feel loved by, someone who has passed away, a beloved friend, or a spiritual figure. It could even be an animal or an inanimate object. The loving presence should bring about feelings of peace, safety, and love.
6. Focus on the loving feelings this presence imparts on you. Feel it warming you from the inside out, or imagine being hugged by this presence allowing the light to penetrate from the outside inward. Allow all these

feelings and positive emotions to be with you in the moment.

7. Let the presence speak affirmations to you, such as saying "You are beautiful," "I love you," or "You make a difference." Don't force this communication, just think about what the person might say to you to help you experience positive vibrations.
8. Put your hand over your heart. Press these enlightening emotions into your body, allowing them to seep through your body and penetrate every cell. Continuously repeat the positive affirmations.
9. Place your arms around your body to embrace yourself in a hug. You could use other physical touches to help you experience the presence too such as stroking your hair, patting yourself on the shoulder, or touching your cheek. Allow yourself to be surrounded by love and light. Let it emerge from your core and radiate from your body.
10. Spend some time in this joyous moment. Once you are ready, slowly open your eyes, and continue your day with this focus on kindness.

Journal

Journaling is a simple mindfulness practice and emotional coping tool. It requires you to write down your thoughts and feelings, which will help you understand yourself better. Many people find that writing assists them in identifying troublesome behaviors, triggers, or deep-rooted emotional issues that require professional help. Identifying emotional problems allows you to work through your thoughts and emotions in a productive manner. Use a dedicated journal for emotional eating. You could even use the same one used as a food diary.

Start the journaling process by writing down your current state, what you are happy about, and any unhappiness. Pay special attention to your feelings and relationships towards food. Your journal is a space for honesty, so write down your true feelings. Do not try to sugarcoat the truth. Repeat this journaling exercise once a week and see how your perspective changes.

Journaling daily is the best way to deal with fluctuating emotions. Make some notes in the morning, before and after meals, and before you go to sleep about your current emotional state, and how it affects your eating. Journal prompts are useful if you do not know what to write about. A prompt is a statement or question that gives you inspiration for your writing. Try some of the following prompts to help you with mindful eating and general mindfulness.

- How hungry are you?
- How do you feel while eating?
- What are your feelings after eating?
- What are your favorite foods and why?
- What did you learn about food during your childhood?

- Write down your perfect day of healthy eating.
- Write down your goals for weight management and your life.
- How has your perception of food changed in the last week, month, or year?
- What bad habits and food relationships do you need to eliminate from your life?
- What are your favorite hobbies or pastimes you could do instead of eating?
- Dear body, I want to embark on mindful eating because...
- I love myself because...

Journaling provides inspiration for future success. It can help you understand yourself better and allow you to accept yourself for who you are while building productive habits. It enables you to have a positive image to work towards and provides motivation for healthy eating.

Make Small Changes

Coping with your emotions requires constant practice just like mindful eating does. It is not an easy process and you need to be kind to yourself along the way. Sometimes, you go full force into a new activity but it becomes unsustainable in the long-term because the change is too big. It is much better to start with small changes and build up to a life of healthy habits. This strategy ensures you master one concept before moving to another one. The ideas below are small changes you can make to help you and you can add some of your own ideas as you see fit.

A Month of Mindful Eating

Commit to being aware of your emotions for one month. As soon as you start to think about food, write down how you are feeling before you eat and after you have eaten. Make notes about your emotions, when and where you experience them, and why. Write down what you want to eat and what you decided to eat. Do this every time you are prompted to eat.

Choose an Emotion

Check your notes from the month, and identify the emotion that comes up most frequently. You only need to choose one emotion. The others will have a turn at a later stage. For this exercise, let's use stress as the main emotion in the notes.

Find Coping Strategies

Determine how you can deal with this emotion in a healthy way. For example, you could deal with stress through meditation, exercise, or reading instead of eating.

Focus on the Trigger

Whenever you feel the urge to eat, identify the predominant emotion at that time. This emotion is triggering your eating, so if you identify it as stress (for example), then move on to the next step.

Use the New Technique

After identifying the trigger as the reason you want to eat, it is time to take action. Bring your list of coping strategies for this emotion into play, even if it is just for a short while. For example, you could do the relaxation meditation, go for a brisk five-minute walk, or read a couple of pages from your favorite book. Allow the new technique to take the place of eating until the urge to eat passes.

Get Support

Involve your family and friends in your emotional and weight loss journey. It helps to find an accountability partner with whom you can talk to daily about how you fared with the emotion you are treating. Many times, an accountability partner can help you through your emotion, if you call upon them when you struggle to practice the coping strategy. They can talk to you for a few minutes or go on a walk with you to help distract you from your emotional craving.

Repeat

Once you have one emotion under control (about a month later), repeat the process with the next most prevalent emotion on your list. Remain patient, you can succeed.

Take Five

Mindless eating becomes an automatic event, but you can stop it if you press pause for a few moments. Stop in your tracks whenever a craving hits or you feel like eating. While you are paying attention to yourself, you can consider why you have a craving and decide to take a different course of action. The most important thing is to take five minutes, that is all.

Ask yourself whether you can wait to eat for five minutes. If that seems like too big a challenge, then wait for one minute, and another minute, and another, until you reach five minutes. Be patient with yourself, and continuously request yourself to wait. It's not that you won't eat, you just need some time to think before you eat.

Check-in with your emotions and hunger while you take five. Determine your prevailing emotions, measure your hunger on the relevant scale, and try to find a different way to deal with the craving. Write down these emotions and other information, especially if you do decide to eat something, so that you can understand your decision later on.

Do Something Else

What would you do if you cannot eat right now? Try to name at least five things you could do instead of eating and write them down in your journal. The easiest way to overcome mindless eating is to do something else when you want to eat. Here are several things you could do when a craving hits.

Visualize

Your imagination is a powerful tool. Use it to entertain yourself and distract you from food cravings.

- Visualize yourself full of energy.
- Imagine yourself at your dream weight.
- Paint a picture of bliss.
- Visualize a healthy meal.
- Think about your dreams for the future.

Get Moving

When you move, you release the same feel-good hormones as when you are eating. Start moving and feeling good without the guilt of food.

- Take a walk around the block.
- Dance.
- Play an instrument.
- Wash your car.
- Do some gardening.
- Fit new clothes.

Spend Time with Others

Socialization is an excellent way to bust cravings. It gives you time to think of something else than food.

- Call a friend.
- Read a book to children.
- Volunteer at a local charity.
- Play a board game.
- Attend an event.

Look After Yourself

Self-love is essential if you want to move forward on your weight management journey. Appreciate your body and who you are by taking care of it properly.

- Go for a massage.
- Thank yourself for your hard work.
- Take a nap.
- Go for a manicure and pedicure.
- Buy flowers for yourself.

Express Yourself

Don't bottle up your emotions, instead, let them out. When you release emotions, you set yourself free.

- Write down your top ten reasons to exercise.
- Journal.
- Scream.
- Write a thank you note to someone.

- Pray.

Declutter Your Life

An organized life leads to an organized mind. Start to sort out the clutter around you, and it will have a positive mental effect.

- Fold the laundry.
- Wash the dishes.
- Write down a to-do list.
- Plan your vacation.
- Create a meal plan.
- Clear a junk drawer.
- Complete an unfinished project.
- List your priorities and goals.

Choose your favorite options from the lists above. Make a shortlist with your top five to ten ideas and carry it with you wherever you go. Pull out your list as soon as you feel a craving, and put your distraction tactics to the test.

Ideas for Specific Emotions

All these activities may seem a little overwhelming and abstract at first. It helps to have ideas for when you experience specific emotions so that you have a quick strategy to deal with your cravings. Here are some ideas.

Stress

Start exercising to get your blood pumping. Break fitness down into a set number of squats, push ups, burpees, or star jumps at a time. Try jogging, cycling, or swimming if you want to put distance between yourself and the stressful event. Yoga or pilates provides a challenge and improves awareness, as it requires your full concentration. Do a meditation exercise, go for a neck and shoulder massage, breathe deeply, and drink lots of water.

Celebrations

When you achieve something amazing you want to celebrate, and you should, but don't turn to food. Find another reward. Treat yourself to a new outfit or hobby equipment. Feed your emotion with an adrenaline-filled activity, like rock climbing or mountain biking. Take a bubble bath, have sex, or go for a beauty treatment.

Seeking Comfort (Loneliness, Sadness, and Depression)

After a long day or difficult event, there is nothing better than a bowl of your favorite comfort food. Now, is the time to change this habit, and find other ways of getting comfort. Ask a friend to come over for a chat, give someone a hug, and watch a feel-good movie. Snuggle up in your favorite blanket, or play with your pets. Meditate or do yoga. Have a cup of tea. Find solace in nature and watch a sunset. A candle-lit bubble bath with soft background music does a world of good.

Boredom

Mindless eating occurs when you are bored, so it is time to ditch this feeling. Make a list of things you have been putting off and want to get done. Choose one item off this list each time you feel bored, and complete this task when you identify boredom. Clean your room, sort out your closet, wash the car, or do some filing. Change rooms and spend some time reading, painting, or journaling. Listen to music, call a friend, or get some exercise.

Socialization

Eating and socializing are frequent partners, so you need to get your social circle to help you out with this one. Choose something else to do than eat. You could play a team sport, go for a hike or bike ride, or go dancing. Consider going bowling, attending a paint night, or watching a movie. Walking with friends during your lunch hour is helpful, and challenge each other to attend charity fun runs.

Towards a Positive Future

Mindfulness assists you to cope with problems in an effective and healthy manner. Using the strategies in this chapter, you will reduce negative thoughts while increasing your self-confidence. Mindfulness will help you to gain control over your life, decrease overwhelming feelings, and allow you to identify eating triggers. Use these coping mechanisms frequently and as a collaborative tool with mindful eating.

Chapter 8: Mindfulness and Eating Disorders

Eating disorders refer to an array of psychological conditions resulting in the development of unhealthy eating habits. It could start as a food obsession, food aversion, issues with body weight and shape. Many people hide their eating disorders because they fear judgment by others, but leaving these disorders untreated can lead to detrimental health and even death in extreme cases. Consult a doctor if you think you have an eating disorder so that they can help you get your health back on track.

Mindfulness is a popular part of treatments for eating disorders. It is useful to help you focus on the positive things and assists in separating your psychological state from your eating habits. Both binge eaters and emotional eaters benefit from mindful eating practices.

Binge Eating

Binge eating is a prevalent eating disorder and one that you might not realize you have. A binge refers to a period of time in which you consume a lot of food in an attempt to escape your emotions. About

70% of obese individuals engage in binge eating, but mindful eating can decrease binge eating by more than 50% (Bjarnadottir, 2019). Binge eating is different from overeating since binge eating occurs even when a person isn't hungry at all. Soon after a binge, you will feel guilty or ashamed about your actions.

Symptoms

There are various signs of being a binge eater. You might sneak snacks, sometimes a whole grocery run full, into your room, eat them in secret, and then hide the evidence. Another example is buying a cake for friends but finishing it alone, which is followed by guilt. You might find yourself ordering three meals and a milkshake from a fast food restaurant and eating everything, resulting in feelings of uncomfortable fullness. This is different to occasional overeating, which could be seen as mindlessly eating a large popcorn during a movie.

Other symptoms of binge eating include:

- Eating until you feel uncomfortably full
- Eating alone to avoid embarrassment
- Eating very quickly
- Eating without hunger cues
- Experiencing sadness, loneliness, guilt, and disgust

If you find yourself eating vast amounts of food in a short time and feel that this behavior is out of control, then you need to consider your situation carefully. Binge eaters need instant gratification and, although you might consume food so quickly it becomes mindless, you need the food to feel better about yourself, even if it is for a very short time. You may have a binge eating disorder if you binge at least once weekly for longer than three months.

Reasons for Binge Eating

There are many reasons why a person may become a binge eater. Some reasons are based on emotional issues while others have their roots in family matters. Whatever the reason for your binge eating, you need to address the situation immediately to get your health back.

Genes

Binge eating can become a family affair, as it could be part of your genetics. If a parent or grandparent was a binge eater, then you may have the same binge eating gene, which increases your chances of falling victim to this eating disorder. The genes responsible for binge eating cues affect networks in your brain that normally control mood and appetite. Having a binge eating gene does not mean that you will become a binge eater—this disorder has to be triggered by something else.

Copycat Eating

Your family and upbringing affect your eating habits. Adults set an example for children, so your binge eating may have been something you learned from family members. Be very careful if you have children or other individuals looking up to you; you don't want to influence their eating habits negatively. Binge eating must be treated, but if you are struggling, then do not binge in front of impressionable individuals.

Extreme Dieting

Diets place restrictions on your food choices and consumption, which later leads to binge eating. When following a diet, you may have to skip meals, eat too little, or really just need a cheat day. Instead of treating yourself, you could find yourself binge eating everything not allowed on your diet plan. Of course, this results in guilty feelings and you may find yourself eating even more.

Depression

A link between depression and binge eating does exist, but the exact cause-and-effect is still murky. Researchers are trying to understand whether guilt and shame from binge eating cause depression, or whether it is the other way round. Regardless, approximately half of binge eaters also have depression, so consider it a warning sign if both are present in your life.

Stress and Anxiety

Traumatic or stressful events can lead a person to overeat. Usually, this is a short-term occurrence, and the person returns to healthy eating habits once the stress is removed. You might have experienced overeating before tests or after losing a friend. This relates closely to emotional eating. If this situation is left untreated or if you let it get out of control, you may find that you frequently binge at the smallest sign of stress.

Low Self-Esteem

When you are unhappy about your body, you feel bad about yourself, which leads to low self-esteem. This could be the result of your own beliefs or something that someone else had said. Browsing through social media and magazines doesn't help the situation either, because the media portrays bodies differently from what they look like in reality. Low self-esteem may cause binge eating and extreme guilt resulting in a downwards spiral.

Binge eating remains a health risk and has many complications. If you binge, you may experience anxiety, depression, and other psychological problems. You also increase your risk of developing diabetes, hypertension, and heart disease, which makes you susceptible to stroke and organ damage.

Mindful Eating to Overcome Binge Eating Disorder

Binge eating results in negative emotions after rapid, excessive eating. In contrast, mindful eating focuses on the eating experience and moderation. Mindfulness is an ideal treatment for binge eating. It allows you to see yourself objectively while remaining aware of the current moment. Mindfulness breaks down the protective barriers you set up with binge eating and enables you to see recovery in a healthy manner. Mindful eating allows you to see food as a nutritional tool rather than as a coping mechanism. In turn, you can deal with your binge eating triggers in an effective manner.

Mindfulness can help you to overcome binge eating by reducing negative thoughts and enables you to build your confidence through proper eating. If you are a binge eater or feel a binge eating episode coming on, then you could follow the next steps to help you become a healthy, mindful eater.

Recognize Your Hunger

Use the hunger scale frequently during the day to help you establish if how hungry you are at that moment. Eat something as soon as you rate your hunger as a three or four. Avoid reaching the one or two-level, because you will be so hungry by that time that you will be more likely to overeat, which could result in binging. Evaluate your hunger after 15 to 20 minutes of eating, and stop when you reach a level six or seven. If you still feel hungry, then allow 15 minutes to pass before you eat something else. You might find you now feel full and won't fall prey to binging.

Remove Binge-Worthy Foods

You probably have a list of favorite foods for binging. It could be chocolate, cake, chips, a fast food meal, ice cream, or something else. Clear your house of all these foods so that you do not become tempted through cravings.

Concentrate on Your Food

Use as many mindfulness techniques while eating as possible. Switch off devices and screens to avoid becoming distracted, sit at the table to eat, and do not try to multitask while eating.

Use a Food Journal

Write down all the foods you eat and how you feel when eating. Study your food journal for triggers. It also helps you identify if you really ate too much or whether this is a figment of your imagination.

Replace Boredom With Activity

Boredom frequently leads to binge eating, especially if you are alone and start to feel sad or depressed. Find activities to do in your spare time instead of lying around at home. Being productive makes it easier to remain positive and doesn't leave time for binge eating.

Binge eating is a serious food disorder that can point to underlying emotional or psychological issues. Once you deal with these problems you can overcome binge eating. Mindful eating is the ideal lifestyle change if you struggle from binge eating because you can still enjoy your favorite foods albeit in a more responsible way.

Emotional Eating

Emotional eating occurs when you decide to cope with your emotions by eating. Some people refer to this situation as, "eating their emotions" because they are not hungry physically but they seek comfort from food. This "comfort" actually comes from the release of feel-good hormones in the biological loop.

Symptoms of Emotional Eating

You probably have a good idea if you are an emotional eater because you know you reach for food when your emotions ride a rollercoaster. You may eat when you are stressed, sad, anxious, bored, happy, angry, or other emotions. You eat in the hope of feeling better, as you believe it will calm you down or make you happier. Emotional eaters use food as a reward for doing something good, or as a reward for getting through a tough situation. You may eat even if you are not hungry and you could be eating after you reach satiation. Food might be a safe haven for you, a friend who supports you when you need emotional help.

Causes of Emotional Eating

Emotional eating doesn't just happen. There is some precursor that causes you to grab food to deal with your emotions. At its core, it is an emotion that triggers this compulsive behavior, but understanding what causes this emotion will help shed light on your choices.

Childhood Habits

Most of your habits in adulthood come from what you were taught as a child. Your parents might have rewarded you for a good school term by taking you for ice cream, gave you a candy bar after falling, or purchased takeaways for the family if a parent had a busy day. All of these actions were done with good intentions, but they taught you that eating when emotional is okay. Now, you repeat the same actions in your adult life.

Stress

Stress can make you more hungry resulting in overeating. Chronic stress generates a hormone called cortisol, which produces cravings for sweet, salty, and fried foods. All of these foods allow for a quick release of feel-good hormones and provide energy. If you cannot control your stress, then you will be at risk for emotional eating.

Numbing Emotions

Emotional eating is an avoidance behavior. When you experience unwanted emotions, you may decide to eat something, rather than face your emotional instability. Ignoring your emotions is not the solution to your problems. You need to address the real situation to set yourself free from emotional eating.

Feeling Empty

Sometimes, you feel as if you have a void in your life. This could be due to boredom or feeling empty. If you experience this emptiness, then you might decide to fill it with food. Eating is a distraction when you feel you have no purpose or are uncertain about how to achieve satisfaction.

Social Influences

Social settings easily cause overeating and emotional eating. You may become nervous or stressed in social circles and start to eat as a coping mechanism. The excitement and happiness of spending time with others can elicit great joy too, which may lead to celebratory eating.

It is always a good idea to determine the cause(s) of your emotional eating. It helps you to address the real problem, and you can identify emotional triggers. Identifying the cause might not happen overnight, and it could be quite complex, but the investigation will increase your mindfulness.

Emotional Eating Cycle

Food can be used as a reward or a pick-me-up on occasion. It is not a problem if you do it this way, but you cannot let it become a compulsive behavior. If eating becomes your primary coping mechanism for emotional circumstances, then you may soon face the perpetual emotional eating cycle.

There are four steps in the cycle:

- You become upset about something.
- You have an overwhelming craving for food.
- You overeat, even though you know better.
- You feel ashamed and guilty.

This cycle continues on and on. You can start at any point in this cycle and will soon realize that you circle on to the other steps. It is very difficult to get out of this cycle, and you will beat yourself up because it feels like you are failing. The only way to escape this vicious cycle is to learn better ways to cope with your emotions. Mindfulness is one strategy to help you overcome emotional instability.

Difference Between Emotional Hunger and Physical Hunger

A big problem with emotional eating is that people do not recognize it as emotions, but rather assume it is hunger. Separating emotions from hunger is essential if you want to overcome emotional eating. The differences between these concepts may seem a bit vague in your daily life, but mindful eaters become more aware, and this will help you identify what you are really experiencing.

Here is a comparison.

- Emotional hunger starts quickly while physical hunger builds gradually.
- Emotional hunger presents as thoughts of eating whereas physical hunger manifests within your stomach.
- Emotional hunger appears as sharp, incessant cravings while physical hunger generates growling sounds that occur off-an-on.

- Emotional hunger is satisfied by certain foods, textures, or tastes, while physical hunger is satisfied by any food, even ones you do not prefer.
- Emotional eating is challenging to satisfy, and most people eat too much, but physical hunger only requires a regular portion of food to feel satisfied.
- Emotional eating may result in feelings of shame, regret, and guilt after eating, whereas physical hunger doesn't cause negative feelings.

Become Mindful of Your Emotions

Mindfulness can help you sort through your emotions. It allows you to become aware of what you are feeling without judgment and to embrace these emotions. Here is a technique for emotional mindfulness:

- Take a few deep breaths.
- Tell yourself: "It is okay to feel (insert emotion)."
- Name the emotion and welcome it into your being, even if it has negative qualities.
- Remain neutral in your attitude towards the emotions, but have a sense of curiosity and kindness.

- Ask the emotion what it wants from you and truly listen to the requests from your inner being.
- Thank the emotion for sharing these insights, and tell it you will work on improving the situation.
- Take a few deep breaths and then continue with your next activities.

This quick exercise enables you to tune into your body's needs. It allows your body to find peace and ensures it that you will protect it in other ways, rather than creating a defense through food. You can also use this process as writing prompts for your food journal.

Feeding Your Feelings

Becoming a mindful eater is an excellent choice if you struggle with emotional eating. There are so many mindful eating activities and tools that can help you determine whether you experience physical or emotional hunger, and these tools can help you beat your emotional cravings. Overcoming emotional eating is a challenge, but you can do it with determination and grit.

As you start out on mindful eating, you have to realize that you won't always be able to say no to emotional eating. There will be times when you find yourself searching for food because nothing else brings you satisfaction. When this happens, you should keep in mind three principles. These three principles will help you to remain a mindful eater during emotional eating episodes.

1. Accept that emotional eating is a choice you make to help you cope with a situation. Coping is not a failure, so emotional eating cannot be a failure either, and no reason exists to feel guilty.
2. Follow the mindful eating principles when you eat emotionally. This means you have to eat with awareness, remain in the moment, sit at the table, avoid other distractions, and so on. The eating period should have an identifiable start and finish times to avoid mindless eating.
3. Emotional eating does not require overeating. Stop eating when your hunger level is at a five or six on the hunger scale.

Emotional eating can help you to overcome a current situation if you remain mindful throughout the process. Mindful eating should become a ritual that you can apply regardless of your circumstances because it focuses on awareness. Use your mindful eating techniques to slow down your snowballing emotions, so that you eat sensibly and without feelings of shame or guilt.

Conquer Emotional Eating

Deciding to change from an emotional eater to a mindful eater is a big step. You should be proud of yourself for wanting to cope with your emotions better and in healthier ways. Finding alternative coping strategies is important if you want to replace emotional eating once and for all. Whenever you feel a bout of emotional eating coming on, take a moment to identify the underlying emotion. Once you name the motion, you can use a suitable technique to cope. If you feel lonely or depressed, then doing something to lift your spirits like reminiscing about a good time with friends, paging through a photo album, or playing with your pets. Deal with anxiety and stress by transferring your nervous energy through dancing, mediation, yoga, or clenching a stress ball. Exhaustion can be overcome by taking a hot shower or bath, using aromatherapy and essential oils, drinking a cup of tea, and taking a nap.

Beat Eating Disorders

Any change in eating habits is difficult, even more so when the habit is part of your very existence and a means of coping. Eating disorders have no place in your life, so take back control of your eating and beat binge and emotional eating. Keep a positive attitude, immerse yourself in other activities, and congratulate yourself for the small victories. You have all the power within you to transform your life, and mindfulness can help you manifest this strength to manage your eating behaviors.

Chapter 9: Mindful Eating and Weight Loss

Weight loss is a hot topic in most conversations. Everywhere you go, you will hear people talking about their weight and how they are attempting to lose a few pounds for this reason or that event. Society constantly pushes the idea of the "perfect" size, but it is unrealistic and only leads to unhealthy eating behaviors.

Think about yourself and your close social circle for a moment. Identify some destructive weight loss behaviors they exhibit. Some people skip meals, decide to fast, or only eat cauliflower and chicken for a month. There are hundreds of fad diets and so-called "quick fixes" that promise weight loss in the blink of an eye. This is unrealistic and unhealthy.

You have to feed your body properly if you want to be healthy. Yes, you might be able to cut down on portion sizes, your sugar, and caffeine consumption, and limit your snacking. All of these things are good, but you can do all of these things in moderation and without restriction through mindful eating. Mindful eating works because it changes your cognitive behavior and lifestyle rather than saying what you can and cannot eat.

Mindful Eating Versus Dieting

How many diets have you been on where you lost the weight and kept it off?

Very few people manage to use short-term diets for long-term weight loss. About 85% of individuals who lose weight by dieting will regain the weight lost (plus a few extra pounds) mere years after their efforts. In contrast, studies using mindful eating found that obese individuals lost weight at a healthy rate and did not regain any weight in subsequent months. Most participants were able to maintain their weight or lost a few more pounds (Bjarnadottir, 2019). Mindful eating is much better than dieting because it changes your approach and behavior towards food while reducing eating-related stress. Mindful eating works since it improves your relationship with food rather than restricting it.

Diets believe that weight loss is possible through willpower alone. You have to use self-discipline to stick to a limited list of foods, ignore your cravings entirely, and only eat at certain times, which will allow you to lose weight. This is wishful thinking. You may be able to cope with the diet mentality for a few days or weeks, but at some time you are going to be emotional, have a craving, or need the energy to continue with your day. You wouldn't deny food to a five-year-old child who says they are physically hungry, yet diets expect you to deny food to yourself, even when you experience real physical hunger.

The problem with diets is that they set high expectations, give you a list of do's and don'ts, but then leave you hanging. Diets label food as food or bad, which causes you to believe that choosing the wrong food makes you a "bad" person. There is no further support to help you through days when your diet is challenging. They don't teach you to cope with your cravings or how to make healthy eating a long-term habit.

Mindful eating is the total opposite of a diet. It is a loose concept focused on eating with awareness. You can eat whatever you want whenever you want as long as you remain mindful of the experience and eat in response to your physical cues. Mindful eating encourages you to listen to what your body needs and respond accordingly. By focusing on internal messages, you increase your awareness and you manage to eat just what you need to satisfy yourself. You allow your body to tell you when it is full, and you have tools like the hunger scale to help you understand these prompts. Mindful eating can help you to lose weight and see food for what it is, a nourishing resource.

Losing weight successfully is an elusive activity. Diets are challenging, especially when you consider how many there are and the variety of their rules. It is tough to decide on the best diet for your body and health concerns. The best diet seems to be the one the media currently advertises, and that can change tomorrow. Some weight loss programs focus on goal setting, like saying you should lose ten pounds in six weeks while others take a behavioral approach and require that you make small adjustments to your eating on a daily basis. Diets may emphasize eating a set number of calories, and require frequent exercise, but both these requirements start to seem like a punishment after a while.

Mindful eating is a bridge between different diets. It places the control in your hands since you know yourself best. It encourages awareness of calories, eating more healthier foods while having smaller portions of special treats, and uses activity including exercise as a way to cope with your cravings and emotions. By concentrating on the journey from mindless eating to mindful eating, you start to realize that the beliefs of diets do have a purpose, but you apply them in a healthier way that is suitable to your personal tastes.

Weight Loss Versus Well-Being

When you decide to lose weight intentionally, you are forcing your body and mind to change their internal processes. This process is called adaptive thermogenesis and alters your psychology, physiology, and biology. Your body is used to maintaining a body fat level based on your nervous system, but you are pushing this storage system to change with intentional weight loss. This sudden change in diet is not something your body takes to kindly, which means it will easily reverse the process if you slip up with your diet.

The changes described above are metabolic in nature, but your body has to adapt biologically too. Your body will resist these immediate changes by altering its chemical balance. For example, restricting your food may cause increased cravings and simultaneously decrease leptin, which is the hormone responsible for feelings of fullness. Additionally, restrictive diets result in distractibility, irritability, and intense emotional responses, especially binge eating and consuming food when not hungry.

The other problem with restrictive diets is that it relies on external information. You learn to eat a set list of foods at certain times, and you have to follow rules set by someone that does not know what your body is experiencing. All of these factors are external to your body. Through this process, you start to distrust the cues from your own body and no longer realize what it is trying to say. You need to relearn how to be self-efficient and trust yourself, which will help to improve your self-esteem.

The best way to get to know yourself is through mindfulness. Mindfulness takes the focus away from weight loss and directs your attention to wellbeing at both a physical and psychological level. It teaches you to look internally for cues about food and to seek new ways to satisfy your real carings. Even if you do not lose weight with mindful eating, your general well-being improves. This leads to general health improvements because you no longer consume less healthy foods in large amounts and you don't overeat. You may find that you have lower cholesterol and blood glucose levels, shorter bouts of depression, fewer food cravings, and a generally positive outlook. These are just some of the benefits you get from focusing on wellbeing rather than on weight loss.

Overeating Triggers

Weight loss with mindfulness is possible, but you need to make changes at the foundation. Being aware of your current situation is one of the best ways to turn from mindless into mindful. It allows you to identify eating triggers, which lead to overeating. At its core, mindless eating resulting in weight gain is due to overeating. Once you identify your overeating triggers, you can limit your exposure to these elements, and start to regain mindful control.

There are three main triggers you should be aware of for mindless overeating.

Distraction

Being distracted is a major factor in overeating. You might not realize how much you eat while you are watching TV, busy with work, or browsing social media. Even general dinnertime conversation can distract you from your food. You need to identify any distractions when eating so that you can address them now. Write down a list of these distractions in a food journal. If you don't enjoy writing, then give yourself a visual cue to distractions by using sticky notes. Place a sticky note on anything that could be a distraction while eating—for example, your cellphone, a wall calendar, an unfinished painting, etc. When you do sit down for a meal, position yourself away from these distractions so that your full attention is on your food.

Emotions

Your emotional state will affect your weight loss efforts. Different emotions affect the hormonal balance in your body even if you are eating only what you should in limited amounts, the hormones in your body could prevent weight loss because the hormones are a defense mechanism. You need to deal with your emotions first, and your weight loss will follow. Go over the section on emotional eating in the previous chapter to help you with this trigger.

Environment

The space you are in at any time of the day could have external cues that entice you to eat. You could be sitting in the car without a morsel of food, look up and see a billboard advertising a bar of chocolate, and end up stopping at the store to buy one. While watching TV and browsing social media you see posts about food and eating. In your own home, you may be confronted with food, even from something harmless such as a photo of a social gathering at a restaurant. Identify these triggers to eat and make a plan on how you will handle them in the future.

Practical Mindful Eating Tips for Weight Loss

You already learned various mindfulness techniques that you can apply to your life. If your plan is to lose weight, then you should definitely go for it, but do not consider it as a punishment. Start to become fully aware of your decision, and embrace the journey to a healthier slimmer you.

Techniques to Reduce Overeating

A huge part of overeating is eating fast and not getting enough to satisfy your cravings. Here are three techniques to take back control of your eating habits. They will help you to become more aware and give your body enough time to send fullness cues which means you stop eating sooner.

Eat In the Dark

A large part of awareness during eating comes from visual cues. You can see how much food you have on your plate, the type of foods, and the colors. Take away your sense of sight to enhance the rest of your senses. You can eat an entire meal in the dark at night, close your eyes for a few bites, or use a blindfold. When you cannot see what is on your plate, you have to rely on your taste buds to give you information. You are less tempted to eat everything because you have to eat slower, which allows you to realize satiation cues. Eating in the dark could lead to much smaller portion sizes, and you can use this as an indicator for future portions.

Switch It Up

You eat faster and more when you have the right utensils. Changing your utensils entirely, as seen in Chapter Six, can help you to eat slower and be more aware of your eating. Do this frequently if you are overeating and want to lose weight.

A Taste Bud Curveball

The first bite of food always tastes amazing, but subsequent bites lose this effect. This leads to eating more because you seek the same experience you had with the first bite. Your taste buds start to recognize the taste and get used to it, so eating the rest is less appealing, yet you continue to eat in search of satisfaction. If you experience this, take a bite of a different food that has another temperature, texture, or flavor. Wait a few seconds, then return to the first food and take another bite. Determine if it tastes different and now satisfies you. If it doesn't, then accept that you won't have the same experience as the first bite and walk away from this food item.

Interview With Yourself

Mindfulness requires a keen interest in yourself and the communication given by your body. When you are trying to lose weight, you are constantly faced with wanting to eat and need to learn your body's cues to understand what it really wants. This situation takes time and practice. One way to help you build a sense of hunger knowledge is to have an interview with yourself whenever you feel the urge to eat. You can also use this strategy if you already put food into your mouth mindlessly, as it will help understand what drove you to this action.

The main question you want to answer is why you are eating. You need to investigate whether you are hungry. This is very difficult to know because the chances of experiencing real physical hunger are very slim since it isn't something you are exposed to frequently. There are three questions that can help you understand your hunger and whether you should be eating.

1. Do I Need To Eat?

If you really need to eat, then you will experience physical hunger cues. You either need energy through calories, macronutrients from proteins, fats, and carbohydrates, micronutrients like vitamins and minerals, or a combination of these. When you need to eat, you could have physical cues such as tiredness, a rumbling stomach, or dizziness. These signals should alert you to the fact that eating cannot be put off any longer.

2. Do I Want To Eat?

If you simply want to eat, it is usually because you are craving something that tastes good. Your craving could be for something that is not nutritious and loaded with salt, sugar, and fat. An enjoyable or favorite flavor and texture could be right at the top of the list. You will have a sudden desire to eat these foods, so wait a few minutes for the craving to pass. If you do give in to temptation, then take a very small portion and consume it mindfully.

3. Do I Feel Like I Should Eat?

There are some situations where you feel that you should be eating, but you may not be hungry at all. Question whether your current environment or external cues are the reason behind eating in this case. You do not need to conform to social norms, so rather turn to a different activity or measure your hunger on the appropriate scale before eating unnecessarily.

Some Other Ideas

Here are some more ideas and tips to help you with your weight loss efforts. All of these ideas promote mindfulness.

Get Enough Sleep

Sleeping too little makes you hungrier and you are more likely to eat when you wake up. Sleep at least eight hours per night. Practice mindfulness before you go to bed to help you focus on sleeping. Switch off all digital devices, do relaxation exercises or meditation, and be grateful as you lay down to sleep. When you do wake up the next morning, take a moment to be thankful for the new day, and evaluate your hunger using the hunger scale before deciding to grab a snack for mindless munching.

Meal Plan

Planning your meals is a good way to improve your mindfulness. It gives some structure to your food choices and helps you to know what you are going to eat. If you have an idea of what you can eat on a specific day, you will eat smaller portions and be less prone to snacking because you don't have to wonder about what you are going to eat. Use your meal plan to write a grocery list, and only purchase the food items on your list in reasonable amounts. Prepare the food once you get home by cutting up vegetables, marinating meat, and so on. By preparing your food in advance and portioning it properly, you become less tempted to grab something quickly or out of convenience. Pre-portioning also helps you to eat less, and you can always use the two-plate approach if you think you are still overeating.

Eat More Plant-Based Foods

Vegetables have fewer calories, so bulk up on them if you feel you need to eat a bit more. A cup of cucumber has almost no calories compared to several hundred in a cup of pasta. You should avoid overeating at all times. If you eat more vegetables, you can repeat the hunger measurement frequently during your meal and stop eating sooner, which means you are consuming fewer calories but still feel full.

Reward Yourself

You are working hard at being healthier and eating well. Reward yourself occasionally for your efforts by eating something you really love. Buy or prepare it as a much smaller portion and only serve yourself half of what you think you could eat. Enjoy this item while keeping all your mindful eating techniques in place. Stop eating when you feel just a bit full to avoid overeating and try some of the utensil swapping techniques to heighten the experience.

Mindful Eating During Holidays

The holidays and any other celebratory event are a challenge if you are trying to lose weight. You might be one of those people who diet in advance and loses a few pounds so that you can eat more during the holidays. This situation only leads to overeating and feeling ill afterward. It's also very difficult to continue with a diet if you stopped it during the holidays. Mindful eating makes the holidays much easier—it is not a diet, so it is easier to maintain as long as you remain mindful.

Social Strategy

You know the hallmarks of your holidays and what to expect. If your family and friends usually have food at get-togethers, then offer to take a snack platter or dish. You can fill the dish with wholesome, healthy choices, such as carrot and celery sticks, cherry tomatoes, and sliced fruit. Taking a healthy snack platter to an event ensures that you have a healthier alternative if you do get the munchies.

Holidays are full of social distractions, so place yourself as far away from the food and alcoholic beverages as possible. Do not be tempted to talk to the hosts in the kitchen or dining room, and do not get caught up in conversation near a food table. If you do want to talk to someone, then ask them if they could have a walk around the party with you. It will give you some time to move and you purposefully move away from any tempting foods.

Increased Awareness

Keep all your mindful eating strategies in mind beforehand while you attend an event. Evaluate your hunger level, if you feel cravings setting in, and only eat if it is physical hunger. Savor every bite by being aware of the smells, tastes, textures, and colors of the food. It can be challenging to eat mindfully when you are around many people, so it might be easiest to find a quiet area in the garden to eat in peace. If you are having a sit-down meal, then use the two-plate approach, or decide to eat only half of what is on your plate, and reevaluate your hunger before you eat the rest. Be thankful for each item on your plate and put down your utensils between bites which ensures you experience your food fully.

A New You

A healthy body weight is a noble cause because it shows you care about your health and want to improve yourself. Mindful eating allows you to realize this goal by strengthening the connection between mind and body. By focusing more on wellbeing, you empower yourself to make better decisions and start to lose weight through proactive activities. Weight loss can be a slow process but have hope—you will succeed, build a positive self-image, and have a better relationship with eating in the process.

Chapter 10: FAQ

Everything you need to know about mindful eating is in this book. If you are still wondering about some things, then you may find the information below to be useful.

What is Mindful Eating?

Mindful eating forms part of the concept of mindfulness. It means to stay in the moment. With mindful eating, you use various techniques to enhance your awareness of your relationship with food. In turn, this allows you to eat sensibly and in a controlled manner that is beneficial for your health.

Is Mindful Eating a Diet?

No, mindful eating is a practice to increase your awareness of the eating process. It is not a diet, which restricts food or calories. Mindful eating does encourage you to be calorie conscious, consider your food options carefully and eat slower. In the process, mindful eating results in eating healthier and less because you feel full sooner which has similar effects to a diet.

Who Can Become a Mindful Eater?

Mindful eating is suitable for everyone, regardless of age, gender, and other demographic factors. You can teach your children and other family members to become mindful eaters. It is suitable if you have health problems like diabetes and high blood pressure because it generates healthy eating behavior that frequently decreases the extent of your diagnosis. As with any change in your lifestyle, it is advisable to consult a healthcare practitioner before you start practicing mindful eating.

How is Mindful Eating Different From Intuitive Eating?

The concept of mindful eating refers to being aware of what and how you eat. Intuitive eating includes mindfulness, but it is a model with ten principles and three elements. Intuitive eating has more rigid guidelines when compared to mindful eating.

Will Mindful Eating Stop Me From Eating the Foods I Like?

No. You can enjoy any food when you are a mindful eater. The most important thing is to remain aware of the eating process and signals from your body. Mindful eating will help you to determine proper portion size, enhance the sensory experience while eating, and allow you to feel full sooner so you are eating less.

Will Mindful Eating Change My Life?

Mindful eating can change your life as you embark on a journey of sensory stimulation, become one with your body, and have a healthy relationship with food. Mindful eating is part of a large concept called mindfulness. With mindfulness, you are fully present in the current moment and immerse yourself in the experience. Mindful eating will change an aspect of your life while mindfulness will change your whole life.

Can Mindful Eating Cure my Eating Disorder?

Mindful eating can help you overcome eating disorders in a healthy way. It gives you techniques and strategies to understand the underlying causes of your eating disorder and provides tools to help you cope with this problem. Mindful eating is a great way to change your eating habits, but you should always see a doctor about an eating disorder so that they can help you with appropriate treatment.

Can I Lose Weight With Mindful Eating?

Absolutely! Mindful eating practices help you to enjoy food without constant overeating. It teaches you to stay in tune with your body without limiting your choice of or access to food. Have a look at Chapter Nine for more information about weight loss through mindful eating.

What Should I Do if I Forget to Eat Mindfully?

Everyone slips up now and then. Do not punish yourself for this mishap since you are already correcting your behavior by acknowledging mindless eating. Go through the mindful eating activities and exercise in this book to refresh your memory. You can also prepare to eat mindfully with your next meal by printing using the hunger scale, keeping a food journal, and using different utensils. There are so many mindful eating tips that you will soon be back on track.

How Do I Know If I am Eating Mindfully?

Mindful eating is a personal process. If you are doing anything to become more aware of your eating and food, then you are starting to be more mindful. Mindfulness does not happen overnight. You need to practice it daily, even if it is for one meal or a few minutes. The more you use the activities and techniques in this book, the more proficient you will become at mindful eating. The mere fact that you are asking this question already shows that you are thinking about eating differently, which is an indicator of mindfulness. Keep going, you will soon see drastic changes as your mindfulness practices take shape.

I Am Worried About Eating the Wrong Thing. How Can I Prevent This?

There are no right or wrong things in mindful eating. The belief is that all food is good for you, but some foods have better nutritional content than others. For example, pumpkin is a better choice than fried chicken since pumpkin does not contain all the oils and added ingredients that fried chicken does. Mindful eating wants you to be conscious of the calories and nutritional content in your foods, so if a food is high in calories, then the best option would be to eat a smaller portion of it or only eat it on a special occasion.

Whenever you think a food is "wrong," take some time to research the food, its ingredients, and get a rough idea about the calories. Having this information gives you the power to make a suitable decision. You should always follow the mindful eating guidelines, but even more so with a food that is considered to be less healthy. Mindful eating will enhance your experience of the food and make it more enjoyable. Listen to the cues from your body and stop eating when you feel you are starting to become full. Stay focused and celebrate the small achievements.

How Do I Know If I Should Eat?

Are you hungry or do you think you should be hungry? If you aren't hungry, then you don't need to eat. The best way to determine whether you are hungry is to use the hunger scale to measure your hunger level. Only eat if your hunger measures four or less, meaning you are a bit hungry to ravenous. Be wary of eating because societal norms dictate that you should eat at a certain time or because everyone else is eating.

Where Should I Start With the Mindful Eating Process?

First, you should be proud of yourself for deciding to make this change. Reading this book is a great starting point. It will give you the tools to become a mindful eater. Have a look at Chapter Five to become familiar with the mindful eating principles and the basic tools. You can also use Chapter Six for some mindfulness exercises that will help you to make it a part of your daily life. Small changes are all you need to get started on this process, and you can gradually build up to making mindful eating a full-time practice.

How Should I Deal With Cravings?

Cravings are a symptom of a problem just like a sore throat could signify you are getting a cold. You need to identify what your cravings are trying to tell you. Test your craving to determine whether you have physical or emotional hunger. Use the hunger scale to help you decide if you should eat. Alternatively, deal with emotional hunger by identifying the underlying emotion and do an activity to distract you from your craving. You can find some activity ideas in Chapter Seven.

I Really Love Cooking. Can I Still Cook Like I Did Before?

Yes, you can still cook. You might find that your cooking style and ingredient choice changes when you practice mindfulness. You could switch out traditional cooking oil for a healthier alternative, might fry foods less, and opt for healthier cooking methods like grilling, steaming, or juicing. Preparing and cooking food is part of mindfulness because it gives you an appreciation of the raw ingredients and preparation process. Concentrate on the textures and colors of the raw ingredients and how they change while cooking. All of these small things help to increase your mindfulness, so you should continue to cook.

How Do I Remain A Mindful Eater When Going Out?

Keep your mindful eating principles in mind while eating. Only order a small portion, such as a starter, and use the two-plate approach to help you determine how much you should eat. If you are not going out for a meal, but to watch a movie or socialize, then eat something before you go if you are hungry and measure your hunger level when you get to the event. Only eat something if you are still hungry. You will succeed because you already made the choice to improve your life.

Leave a 1-Click Review!

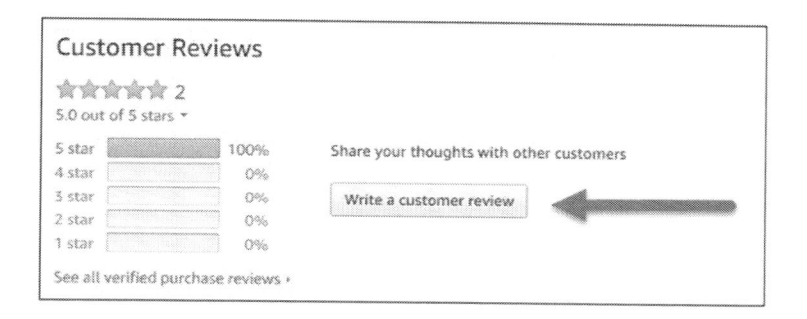

I would be incredibly thankful if you could take just 60 seconds to write a brief review on Amazon, even if it's just a few sentences!

>> Scan with your camera to leave a quick review:

Thank you and I can't wait to see your thoughts.

Conclusion

"When practiced to its fullest, mindful eating turns a simple meal into a spiritual experience, giving us a deep appreciation of all that went into the meal's creation as well as a deep understanding of the relationship between the food on our table, or own health, and our planet's health." - Thich Nhat Hanh, Buddhist monk and peace activist who lives according to mindfulness principles.

How has your life changed since you started the process of becoming a mindful eater?

Visualize your before and after scenarios for a moment, just like you would take before and after photos when on a weight-loss initiative. Create an image titled, "Before Mindful Eating," and another titled "After Mindful Eating." Consider how your life has changed in the process. Your before image might be of yourself and your family eating a whole pizza each while drinking soda and staring blankly at the TV. In your after visualization, you depict your new reality: a family eating together at the table, sharing a single pizza, understanding satiation cues, and talking about the food experience.

Take your visualization one step further. Think about the type of mindful eater you want to be in a year's time. You might see yourself losing weight, being healthier, more energetic, and have a lust for life. Your relationship with food could be even better, you might have planted a few fruits, vegetables, and herbs yourself, and junk food has a very small role in your life. What a great place to be in! Hold onto this vision as you continue to eat mindfully.

Your relationship with food is an important part of your life. It will always be there, so you need to learn how to improve this relationship in a healthy way. Food is an existential piece of our existence. Food is an amazing thing because it comes from the earth, just like you do. You have a connection with the earth through your consumption of food. Every bite of food you take is the sum of nature's efforts. The whole universe—sun, moon, ground, and water—work together to provide amazing produce for you to consume. You should do this with happiness and enjoyment, instead of with feelings of guilt and shame. Once you learn to eat properly through mindful eating, you gain the ability to strengthen your connection to food and the earth.

Mindful eating is the perfect healthy lifestyle choice since it fosters an appreciation for food, rather than restricting your diet. It is healthy to have several food choices. Eating foods with varying textures, tastes, and flavors is healthy. Removing stress from eating is healthy. Enjoying your food is a crucial part of nourishing your body and soul, so a good experience with food is healthy.

The way you prepare your food has a lot to do with how you consume food. Preparing your food is part of the mindful eating experience as it creates appreciation and awareness. It gives you an opportunity to give thanks for nature's creation, and its ability to play a crucial role in your life. As you prepare and eat your food, you satisfy your physical hunger while paying attention to the nurturing qualities of eating in a healthy way. Learning to savor each bite creates a bond between your physical body, food, and your spirit.

Use the mindful eating practices daily, stay focused, and don't beat yourself up about small slip-ups. You have the power within you to change. Once you manifest your healthy eating into daily habits, you give yourself permission to enjoy food fully and without restrictions. These habits become a lifestyle that you can take with you wherever you go, and remain viable regardless of the obstacles you face. Make the decision to change your life today. Make the decision to be healthier and look after your body while eating what you want to eat.

***

Please leave a review for this book if you found the content useful.

If you enjoyed learning about Mindful Eating, but feel the concept is too vague for you, then you might find our other book useful. It is called *Intuitive Eating*. In this book, you will learn about intuitive eating, a similar concept to mindful eating, which has a lot more guidelines for eating healthily. It still allows you to eat what you want and remains a lifestyle plan rather than a diet.

YOUR FREE GIFTS

As a way of saying thanks for your purchase and to help you along your journey towards developing healthier eating habits, we've created free bonus resources that will help you get the best possible results:

Free bonus #1: 30 Common mistakes that can keep you from losing weight
Do you make any of them?

Free bonus #2: The 25 Healthiest Foods You Can Buy for $5 or Less
Eat healthier without breaking the bank

Free bonus #3: Atkins carb counter
Know how many carbs are in the foods you eat

Free bonus #4: Intermittent Fasting for Weight Loss
A beginners guide for women & men to lose your body fat healthy and simply

Free bonus #5: Clean Eating
Staying healthy in a simple way

To get your bonuses, go to

http://bit.ly/NathalieSeaton

or scan with Your camera

References

Ackerman, C.E. (2020). 58 Science-based mindful eating exercises and tips. Positive Psychology. https://positivepsychology.com/mindful-eating-exercises/

Ajmera, R. (n.d.). The effects of poor nutrition on your health. Live Strong. https://www.livestrong.com/article/31172-effects-poor-nutrition-health/

Albers, S. (2017). The surprising benefits of mindful eating. Huffpost. https://www.huffpost.com/entry/mindful-eating_b_1265865

Babauta, L. (n.d.). Dealing with emotional eating issues. Zen Habits. https://zenhabits.net/emotional-eating-issues/

Basso, J. C., McHale, A., Ende, V., Oberlin, D. J., & Suzuki, W. A. (2019). Brief, daily meditation enhances attention, memory, mood, and emotional regulation in non-experienced meditators. *Behav Brain Res. 1*(356), 208-220. https://pubmed.ncbi.nlm.nih.gov/30153464/

Bhandari, S. (2019). Why am I binge eating? WebMD. https://www.webmd.com/mental-health/eating-disorders/binge-eating-disorder/why-binge-eating#1

Bjarnadottir, A. (2019). Mindful eating 101. Healthline. https://www.healthline.com/nutrition/mindful-eating-guide

Chowles, E. (n.d.). Do you need to eat, want to eat, or feel like you should be eating? SleekGeek. https://www.sleekgeek.co.za/2019/02/do-you-need-to-eat-want-to-eat-or-feel-like-you-should-be-eating/

Cleveland Clinic. (2020). The psychology of eating. https://my.clevelandclinic.org/health/articles/10681-the-psychology-of-eating

Cleveland Clinic. (2020). Mindlessly snacking (again)? Try these simple mindful eating exercises. https://health.clevelandclinic.org/mindlessly-snacking-again-try-these-3-simple-mindful-eating-exercises/

Derbyshire Healthy Future Service. (n.d.). The hunger scale. http://www.dchs.nhs.uk/assets/public/dchs/llb//tools/tools_1-11/4_DCHS_A5_4pp_The_Hunger_Scale.pdf

DiR. (2019). 5 Risks and consequences of a poor diet. https://www.dir.cat/blog/en/risks-consequences-of-poor-diet/

Eddins, R. (2018). How to counter emotional eating with mindfulness. The Doctor Weighs In. https://thedoctorweighsin.com/how-to-counter-emotional-eating-with-mindfulness/

Everyday Health (n.d.). 9 Bad eating habits and how to break them. https://www.everydayhealth.com/diet-and-nutrition-pictures/bad-eating-habits-and-how-to-break-them.aspx

Fetters, K.A. (2015). 100 Things to do instead of eating mindlessly. Women's Health.

https://www.womenshealthmag.com/weight-loss/a19902230/avoid-mindless-eating/

FitMind. (2020). Mindful eating: Science and exercise script. https://www.fitmind.co/blog-collection/mindful-eating-exercise-script

Godman, H. (2019). 11 Benefits of mindful eating. U.S. News. https://health.usnews.com/wellness/food/articles/benefits-of-mindful-eating

Halland, B. (2019). 6 Meditations to curb emotional eating. Thrive Global. https://thriveglobal.com/stories/6-meditations-to-curb-emotional-eating/

Hoge, E. A., Bui, E., Marques, L., Metcalf, C. A., Morris, L. K., Robinaugh, D. J., Worthington, J. J., Pollack, M. H., & Simon, N. M. (2013). Randomized controlled trial of mindfulness meditation for generalized anxiety disorder: Effects of anxiety and stress reactivity. *Journal of Clinical Psychiatry 74*(8), 786-792. https://www.ncbi.nlm.nih.gov/pmc/articles/PMC3772979/

Kirkpatrick, K. (2019). 7 Sneaky signs of an unhealthy diet. Cleveland Clinic. https://health.clevelandclinic.org/7-sneaky-signs-of-an-unhealthy-diet/

Kristeller, J. and Bowman, A. (2015). The joy of half a cookie: 9 principles that'll help you eat mindfully. The Mindful World. https://www.themindfulword.org/2015/principles-mindful-eating/

Malacoff, J. (2020). The science behind why eating is so comforting. MyFitnessPal.

https://blog.myfitnesspal.com/the-science-behind-why-eating-is-so-comforting/
May, M. & Johnson, R. (n.d.). Mindful eating - Shifting the focus from weight to well-being. Corporate Wellness. https://www.corporatewellnessmagazine.com/article/mindful-eating-well-being
Mindfulness Exercises. (n.d.). Self kindness - part 1. https://mindfulnessexercises.com/self-kindness-part-1/
Monroe, J.T. (2015). Mindful eating: Principles and practice. American Journal of Lifestyle Medicine. https://journals.sagepub.com/doi/abs/10.1177/1559827615569682?journalCode=ajla#:~:text=The%20basic%20principles%20of%20mindful,to%20assist%20in%20achieving%20awareness.
Prichard, S. (2018). The many benefits of mindful eating. Skip Prichard. https://www.skipprichard.com/the-many-benefits-of-mindful-eating/
Rosenkranz, M. A., Davidson, R. J., MacCoon, D. G., Sheridan, J. F., Kalin, N. H., and Lutz, A. (2013). A comparison of mindfulness-based stress reduction and an active control in modulation of neurogenic inflammation. *Brain, Behavior, and Immunity 27*, 174-184. https://www.sciencedirect.com/science/article/abs/pii/S0889159112004758
Scott, J.R. (2020). What is binge eating? Very Well Mind. https://www.verywellmind.com/when-does-overeating-become-binge-eating-3495807

Smith, M., Robinson, L., Segal, J., & Segal, R. (2020). Emotional eating and how to stop it. HelpGuide. https://www.helpguide.org/articles/diets/emotional-eating.htm

Tamkin, T. (2019). Why science can't seem to tell us how to eat right. Nourish by WebMD. https://www.webmd.com/diet/news/20190422/why-science-cant-tell-us-how-to-eat-right

The Mindfulness Project. (2014). 3 Principles of mindful emotional eating. https://www.londonmindful.com/blog/3-principles-of-mindful-emotional-eating/

The Psych Professionals. (n.d.). Mindful Eating. https://psychprofessionals.com.au/mindful-eating/

Uotani, S. (2019). How to use mindfulness meditation to overcome emotional eating. BetterHumans. https://betterhumans.pub/how-to-use-mindfulness-meditation-to-overcome-emotional-eating-aa95003cfe64

Valentine, M. (n.d.). 20 Mindful eating tips that will transform your relationship with food. Buddhaimonia. https://buddhaimonia.com/blog/20-mindful-eating-tips

Wadyka, S. (2019). How mindful eating can help you lose weight. Consumer Reports. https://www.consumerreports.org/dieting-weight-loss/how-mindful-eating-can-help-you-lose-weight/

White, D.A. (2011). Top 10 worst eating habits. Food Network.

https://www.foodnetwork.com/healthyeats/healthy-tips/2011/03/top-10-worst-eating-habits

The Art of Mindful Eating. (n.d.). The big five benefits of intuitive eating and eating mindfully. https://www.theartofmindfuleating.com/the-5-big-benefits-of-intuitive-eating-and-eating-mindfully/

Zelman, K.M. (n.d.). Why we eat the foods we do. Nourish by WebMD. https://www.webmd.com/diet/features/why-we-eat-the-foods-we-do#1

Printed in Great Britain
by Amazon